Boundaries, Borders
and Frontiers in Archaeology

Boundaries, Borders and Frontiers in Archaeology

A Study of Spatial Relationships

BRYAN FEUER

McFarland & Company, Inc., Publishers
Jefferson, North Carolina

Illustrations and maps by Tina Ross Archaeological Illustrations, www.tinaross.ca.

LIBRARY OF CONGRESS CATALOGUING-IN-PUBLICATION DATA

Names: Feuer, Bryan Avery.
Title: Boundaries, borders and frontiers in archaeology : a study of spatial relationships / Bryan Feuer.
Description: Jefferson, North Carolina : McFarland & Company, Inc., Publishers, 2016. | Includes bibliographical references and index.
Identifiers: LCCN 2015050188 | ISBN 9780786473434 (softcover : alkaline paper) ∞
Subjects: LCSH: Social archaeology. | Spatial behavior—Social aspects—History—To 1500. | Boundaries—Social aspects—History—To 1500. | Borderlands—History—To 1500. | Frontier and pioneer life. | China—Antiquities. | Rome—Antiquities. | Greece—Antiquities.
Classification: LCC CC72.4 .F48 2016 | DDC 930.1—dc23
LC record available at http://lccn.loc.gov/2015050188

BRITISH LIBRARY CATALOGUING DATA ARE AVAILABLE

ISBN (print) 978-0-7864-7343-4
ISBN (ebook) 978-1-4766-2424-2

Front cover image © 2016 iStock

Printed in the United States of America

McFarland & Company, Inc., Publishers
Box 611, Jefferson, North Carolina 28640
www.mcfarlandpub.com

For Lois,
as always

Table of Contents

Preface

This book represents more than thirty years of research concerning boundaries, borders and frontiers, beginning with *The Northern Mycenaean Border in Thessaly* in 1983, which drew upon my dissertation research in that area. Although the focus of my interest has always been the past—and more specifically the Aegean Bronze Age—I draw here upon a wealth of scholarly literature concerning these phenomena within a range of temporal contexts, from contemporary and ethnographic accounts, historical data and archaeological evidence.

In addition to thoroughly exploring the concepts of boundary, border and frontier, I discuss various theoretical and methodological issues concerning peripheries—most notably center/periphery models—as they apply to the archaeological record. After an extensive description and discussion of political, economic, social and cultural processes in border and frontier zones, I conclude with case studies of three societies which exemplify the theories, structures and processes discussed: China, Rome and Mycenaean Greece.

Until fairly recently, archaeological research has been directed primarily toward the cores or centers of societies rather than their peripheries. However, much recent work has begun to redress this disparity of focus. Moreover, borders and frontiers also constitute an extremely interesting and productive subject of research, as I shall demonstrate. Precisely because of their peripheral location, frontiers and borders serve as a locus of interaction between people of varying polities, cultures and ethnicities, resulting, *inter alia*, in a wide range of potential outcomes.

Introduction

Virtually every part of human existence and behavior has a spatial dimension. Humans, like all terrestrial life, require space and resources to exist and to perform activities which, at the minimum, are necessary for survival. Our lives and activities are therefore enacted within a spatial realm which influences them to a considerable degree and, moreover, we envision and structure space in various ways. Space is simultaneously shared and divided; one concept widely employed in respect to attitudes toward space is that of territoriality, the willingness to defend or protect a specified area (Soja 1971:19–20; Mellor 1989:53; Smith 1990:1; Bonzani 1992:210–211).

Implicit in this concept is the idea that space is partitioned so that of the amount of territory potentially available to a group, a portion is restricted to a home or core area that offers security and some degree of separation from others. Thus is created a conflict or dialectic between the need for security and control on the one hand and the opportunity for broader access to space, people and resources beyond the home territory on the other (Gottmann 1973). Territoriality is expressed in most non-human species as well (Soja 1971:32–39). However, not all human groups choose to exercise it to the same extent.

> Territoriality is, therefore, not some innate human trait but a social construct. It can take different forms in different geographical circumstances, and its specific manifestations must be contextualized.... Territoriality and its various expressions must be recognized as means to some end, such as material survival, political control or xenophobia [Smith 1990:3].

In addition to the practical and functional aspects of territoriality, territory includes emotional and symbolic dimensions involving the sense of place and of identity (Smith 1990:2). Territoriality is, as will be shown, closely related to the idea of boundaries.

The study of borders, frontiers and boundaries necessarily entails investigating variation through space. Such variation can be approached by means of various perspectives, derived primarily from the disciplines of geography, history and anthropology (e.g., Sopher 1972; Renfrew 1978; Burnham and Kingsbury 1979:5; Cherry 1987:153). By combining these approaches, I intend here to bring together research and ideas about spatial organization in order to present a theoretical overview of a significant aspect of human cognition and behavior. Although I will draw material from a variety of sources and contexts, my focus here will be upon the expression of spatial behavior and organization and the examination of boundaries, borders and frontiers in an archaeological context. Since the archaeological record is generally less complete in most respects compared to ethnographic or historical contexts, this emphasis will necessitate the discussion of certain methodological issues, including the identification and characterization of boundaries and peripheral zones.

Basic Concepts

Beginning with basic spatial concepts, I first define and discuss the nature and meaning of boundaries, borders and frontiers. After distinguishing between boundaries, which are linear, and borders and frontiers, which are zonal, I then differentiate borders and frontiers, the former constituting the inner edge of the periphery, the latter the outer edge; the significance of this difference will also be discussed. It will be seen from this discussion that while borders have not received a great deal of scrutiny, there is a well-developed literature concerning frontiers. Finally, I consider the relationship among boundaries, borders and frontiers.

Having defined and characterized frontiers, borders, and boundaries, I then examine a number of the theoretical models which have been developed in order to structure, organize and understand spatial relationships. The dominant model is that of center or core and periphery, most notably the world systems approach proposed by Immanuel Wallerstein (1974).

Introduction

Archaeological Implications

Studying the phenomena discussed above in the archaeological record raises a number of methodological issues concerning the identification and characterization not only of boundaries, borders and frontiers, but the processes associated with them. This in turn involves drawing inferences from material remains, particularly in respect to their spatial distribution. I therefore consider the nature of archaeological cultures and whether they in fact exist, concluding that such entities can be recognized (Clarke 1978; Renfrew 1978) and have some meaning not only in terms of social, political and economic organization, but more specifically in respect to boundaries, borders and frontiers.

In order to define past societies or archaeological cultures, scholars have made considerable effort to delimit their boundaries. But as Strassoldo notes, "people largely agree in their identification of the core of things; to find the boundaries is more difficult" (1977:86). The most basic approach has been to use natural boundaries such as rivers and mountains to approximate limits of settlement or control. These natural boundaries have typically been combined with humanly-constructed physical structures of various materials—including wood, earth and stone—most commonly in the form of walls. More recently settlement pattern analysis utilizing central place theory and other geographical constructs have also been used to envision the approximate boundaries of state-level societies (Cherry 1987). A final method has been to map the distribution of artifacts and other items of material culture (Trigger 1974; Hodder and Orton 1976; Feuer 1983; Trinkaus 1984). All of these approaches raise methodological issues, but all of the maps of prehistoric societies published in books and journal articles in fact employ some combination thereof. Of course the accuracy of boundaries thus derived is considerably improved if these projected limits can be combined with any written documentation ranging from inscriptions to ancient texts.

Clearly, distinctions between core and periphery would be difficult to discern in simpler acephalous societies such as tribes, and possibly chiefdoms as well. Thus such characterizations apply almost entirely to state societies which demonstrate some degree of centralization. In such instances it is easiest to begin by identifying the core zone or central region as the area most fully developed along various dimensions

4

such as urbanization, population density, quantity and quality of artifacts, and so on. Peripheral zones would then be defined and characterized in comparison to the center.

Having established a basis for interpreting the archaeological record in respect to spatial considerations, it then becomes possible to consider the dominant theoretical model currently employed in the study of borders, boundaries and frontiers, that of center and periphery, particularly the world systems model proposed by Immanuel Wallerstein and others. Other related models, such as that of increasing or decreasing integration, will also be described.

Various associations accompany the division of space into core and periphery. Most commonly, the core is perceived as superior to the periphery, with all of the connotations and value judgments that typically involve a sense of superiority/inferiority. Since the core is by definition more evolved in various dimensions than the periphery, more highly developed societies almost invariably invoke a contrast between civilization on the one hand and barbarism on the other; although the terms themselves date to the classical age, the attitude surely goes back to the first civilizations, if not earlier (Helms 1988:50; Whittaker 1994; cf. Newby 1983).

> Perhaps the most common (and ethnographically familiar) means of marking such contrasts by territorial differentiation is achieved by recognizing socioterritorial dichotomies or a series of zones, often concentric, to which are attributed a range of sociological or ideological values and characteristics.... Other examples of dichotomies and of zoning (or some aspect thereof, e.g., emphasis on boundaries or thresholds between zones) appear virtually worldwide [Helms 1988:22; cf. Patterson 1977:43].

The perception of "us" vs. "them," seemingly deeply ingrained in human attitudes and behavior, thus consistently assumes a territorial dimension. Ethnic stereotypes are commonly attributed to outsiders and foreigners, often leading to the denial of access to privileges and benefits to those residing beyond the civilized boundary (Kristiansen and Larssen 2005:39). Not only do boundaries—social, symbolic and spatial—recognize, enforce and maintain such separation, but zones of increasing or decreasing integration also often imply greater or lesser degrees of similarity in terms of a wide range of attributes, including sophistication, normality, morality, goodness, ritual purity, and familiarity (Thornton 1982; Helms 1988:23–27, 51; Whittaker 1994:17, 36–37). These divisions between known and unknown are also related to the concept of ecumene (from the Greek *oikumene*), defined by Kopytoff as "a region of persistent cultural interaction and exchange" (1987:10; cf. Kristof 1959; Asiwaju 1986; Armillas 1987). Edmonds also uses this term to describe settled but undeveloped areas within the core that are not strictly peripheral (1985:20; cf. Whitney 1970).

Another aspect of spatial organization concerns interaction among groups within and between areas. Such interactions often, but not always, have a spatial component. Of particular interest in this respect will be interaction which takes place within border or frontier regions or between the core and the periphery. Here the point is that certain kinds of interactions occur more frequently or have a different nature in peripheral zones than in the center and that spatial distribution may influence the nature of such interactions (Ericksen 1980:53; Weber and Rausch 1994:xiv; Lightfoot and Martinez 1995:474).

Evolution of Spatial Concepts and Organization

As human culture evolves changes in the perception of and organization of space occur (Anderson and O'Dowd 1999). The adoption of a sedentary existence and the resulting complexity of social, political and economic organization had a number of demonstrable consequences in respect to spatial organization. As groups became more rooted in one place and as land became more valuable, territoriality, for example, became a much more significant factor in human/land and intergroup relationships. As groups became larger and occupied more territory, greater internal spatial differentiation—into regions and provinces, for example—occurred. And as societies expanded, more significant distinctions between core and periphery emerged as well (Gottmann 1973; Cohen and Maier 1983; Dodgshon 1987).

For hunters and gatherers, the relationship between humans in groups and land was relatively undefined. Groups occupied a territory which they traversed during the course of their nomadic movement and which represented their traditional homeland, but ethnographic studies indicate that they did not have a strong territorial sense about the land itself. Although they primarily inhabited a core area—particularly where gathering was involved and reliable sources of water were available—boundaries either did not exist or were extremely diffuse, and the outer edges of the periphery of their area of exploitation often overlapped with those of other groups (Peattie 1944:57; Bonzani 1992:211). Thus the concepts of core, border, and frontier, though existent, were vague and ill-defined.

Clearly, as groups began domesticating plants and animals and became sedentary, their perception of and relation to territory changed. Land now had a different kind of value and the tie between humans and a specific territory was strengthened. Boundaries between core and peripheral zones tended to be more clearly defined, demarcated and defended, although in tribal and chiefdom-level societies the boundary was more apt to be a buffer zone rather than a linear boundary (Bonzani 1992:213). This concept of territory, however, applies only to settled agriculturalists, since nomadic pastoralists, like hunters and gatherers, had a different notion of territoriality and different land use practices. Pastoralists practiced a more non-exclusive form of occupancy with shifting and diffuse boundaries; such concepts and practices naturally conflicted with those of agriculturalists, particularly at the margins of sedentary habitation (Wilkinson 1983).

Finally, states and state-level societies, more centralized and at the same time more internally differentiated, further elaborated distinctions between core and periphery/peripheries as well as distinctions between peripheries, including more specifically-defined and strongly-defended boundaries (Gottmann 1973:5–6, 138; Mellor 1989:53). Chase-Dunn and Hall, for example, propose that "the stability and exploitativeness of core/periphery hierarchies increases with the degree of stratification within core societies and with the development of certain 'technologies of power,' which enable centralized empires to extract taxes and tribute from peripheral regions" (1991:28). Likewise, "one of the clearest trends in human history has been the formation and integration of political and economic institutions of ever-increasing size" (Feinman and Nicholas 1992:76).

Processes

One of the most interesting and important aspects of peripheral regions concerns the interaction of groups and individuals. Since borders and frontiers inherently involve two or more groups of people coming into contact, such processes, although also of course occurring in core regions, occur more frequently there and often, because of the differences between core and peripheral regions, have a different nature (Lightfoot and Martinez 1995:474). Although boundaries control and filter interaction to some extent, thereby creating discontinuities in contact (often, but not always, reflected in the archaeological record as discussed below), according to the models discussed above, one can observe gradients of interaction as well, particularly along lines of communication (van der Leeuw 1983:18).

Here I will discuss, broadly construed, various social, economic and political processes. Social processes of particular salience in borders and frontiers include aspects of ethnicity, acculturation and intermarriage. Political processes typically involve efforts to control or dominate others, including various forms of conflict. Significant economic processes are acquisition of raw materials, craft production, distribution, trade, and various forms of colonial or imperialist economic exploitation. Although it is often difficult to separate such processes, I will do so here for analytical purposes, and then briefly discuss how such processes are in fact related.

Although social boundaries sometimes coincide with natural or political boundaries, the opportunity or potential for social interaction and mixture is greater in peripheral regions where different cultural and social groups can be found in closer proximity. These interactions enhance the possibility for borrowing and interchange between individuals and groups of people, objects and ideas, processes that have been termed, *inter alia*, diffusion, acculturation, creolization, syncretism and assimilation. Acculturation can be either unilateral (when it is often referred to as assimilation) or mutual, resulting in cultural configurations which blur the boundaries between groups and sometimes lead to the creation of border or frontier cultures which combine elements of contributing or adjacent groups. One form of this interchange is intermarriage, which not only results in biological, racial and ethnic mixtures of various kinds, but also the diffusion and adoption of cultural traits as well. Social and cultural interaction also gives rise to various ethnic processes, including boundary maintenance and ethnogenesis.

Political processes in peripheral regions primarily involve the extension of power and exercise of control, usually of desirable resources such as land, raw materials, and people (as for example, a labor source). Inevitably, efforts to exercise or maintain political control lead to competition and conflict of various kinds, most notably armed conflict. Conflict thereby represents one of the most prominent features of peripheral areas, either between armed groups of varying size from raiding parties to state-supported armies, or on a lower scale, lawless violence. One common form of armed conflict is border disputes, and invasions of territory naturally enough begin at a society's boundary. Since political control is generally weaker and less centralized in frontier zones, with a diffusion or diminution of the monopoly of force, violence and coercion normally exercised by the state, a kind of lawless anarchy often reigns, as occurred perhaps most notably and vividly on the American frontier, but hardly absent in other equivalent circumstances.

As suggested by world systems theory, peripheral regions are and were exploited for raw materials and cheap labor, and particularly in capitalist mercantile economies, were in a dependent relationship with the core area, supplying goods and services and serving as a market for finished and manufactured products. The other primary economic activity or process is trade, with borders or semi-peripheries functioning as intermediaries in economic transactions between the center and peripheral regions, including areas beyond the frontier, i.e., long-distance trade.

Case Studies

To illustrate the concepts and situations I have discussed above, I will describe in some detail several societies which have been studied extensively in respect to them, including the archaeological context with which I am most familiar, Mycenaean Thessaly, which comprised part of the larger "world system" of Late Bronze Age Greece. Mycenaean Thessaly represents but one of the many border and

Introduction

frontier zones throughout human prehistory and history. Although clearly it would not be possible to treat all possible permutations in any depth, I intend to focus on two well-studied instances of similar situations for illustrative purposes, Chinese and Roman civilizations.

1

Boundaries, Borders
and Frontiers

For purposes of clarity, it will be necessary to attempt to define
and understand three widely-used (and sometimes misused) terms/
concepts, i.e., boundary, border and frontier. All three terms have
sometimes been used interchangeably, causing some understandable
confusion in their application (Kristof 1959; Edmonds 1985:18).
Another problem with defining and differentiating these concepts is
that each of them has many alternative meanings, often metaphorical
(e.g., "frontiers of science"), which do not concern the spatial aspects
of human organization discussed here. Not only are there many and
varied definitions, which often overlap but are not exactly the same
(cf. Wittgenstein's "definition" of games), but as will be seen, all of them
have evolved as well. In addition, each term has different meanings,
connotations and nuances in different languages (Gottman 1973:134;
Strassoldo 1977:86).

Boundaries

I begin with the concept of the boundary and boundedness. One
of the most basic distinctions among boundaries, borders and frontiers
is that boundaries are conceived as lines, while borders and frontiers
are characterized as zones (East 1965:98; Chang 1982:5; cf. Elton
1996:127). As such, boundaries represent demarcation, and indicate
certain well-established limits or bounds of a given unit and all that
which lies inside is bound together. Thus the boundary is inner-
oriented, centripetal, while the term frontier has an outer-oriented,

centrifugal meaning, the borderland that is in front of somebody or something, like the *"limes"* of the Roman empire or of Western civilization. That is why the frontier is an integrating, the boundary a separating factor (Malmberg 1980:90; cf. Kristof 1959; van der Leeuw 1983:17; Whittaker 1994:72).

In this sense a boundary marks a limit, and because it by definition separates entities, it follows that the boundary divides one thing from another (Barth 2000:17). Boundaries, even if shifting and movable, can emphasize a more exclusive sense of "us" versus "not us." Boundaries can make the *edge* as important as the *center*. Whereas zones, particularly of the concentric variety, can give a sense of graduated change from the center out toward the periphery, boundaries or thresholds mark the point *within* which proper life is expected to exist, and separate it more definitely from that which lies without. Boundaries try to keep the "good" inside and the "evil" outside. Boundaries keep all eyes turned back, inward toward the center, or, for those who must venture forth, mark the point where ritual protection must begin to safeguard travelers and where purification must take place on their return before they may safely re-enter society (Helms 1988: 28, 31; cf. Cherry 1987:153).

Paradoxically, however, boundaries also are meeting places or junctures between entities, and, like borders and frontiers, therefore represent a locus of interaction. The extent to which any boundary facilitates mixture rather than separation depends to a great deal on its permeability. Boundaries range across a continuum of permeability from totally undefended and wholly open to highly restricted and almost impermeable barriers. The boundaries of the earliest and simplest human societies are examples of the former, but even in the modern world of carefully demarcated and extensively defended state boundaries, there are places which are too remote, difficult or dangerous to function as normal national boundaries, such as the modern Afghanistan-Pakistan or Syria-Iraq borders. Examples of the latter include Hadrian's Wall, the Great Wall of China and the Berlin Wall. However, as the history of these walls clearly indicates, no barrier is capable of entirely preventing the transmission of people, things, and ideas (Cherry 1987:153; Lattimore 1962; Whittaker 1994:8). Most boundaries, naturally, fall somewhere between these extremes, acting as a kind of filter or semi-permeable membrane by admitting some things and rejecting others (Peattie 1944:57; Gottmann 1973:138; Lightfoot and Martinez 1995:473).

Boundaries fulfill various kinds of functions. In addition to marking divisions or distinctions, they often indicate the limits of control or sovereignty as "the outer line of effective control exercised by the central government" (Kristof 1959:272; cf. Ericksen 1980:53). Boundaries enclose people and things, including territory (Malmberg 1980:91). Relatively impermeable barriers or defended boundaries often serve to limit movement, to prevent people or things from entering (e.g., undesirable persons, contraband, etc.).

There are, of course, many different kinds of boundaries (e.g., Rice 1998:47–51), and here I merely wish to suggest briefly some of the most basic and important ones. Boundaries, for example, occur at various levels of human existence and organization. Individuals define boundaries around themselves (commonly referred to as personal space); dwellings (e.g., houses or public buildings) often have defined boundaries, usually expressed in terms of property lines and/or fences or other barriers; communities usually have delineated boundaries, such as city limits; and polities, particularly states, have clearly defined and demarcated boundaries (Soja 1971). It is this highest level, of the polity, that I shall be concerned with here.

Another distinction of some significance is that between social and physical boundaries (van der Leeuw 1983:17). Social boundaries tend to be symbolic, conceptual and/or ideational. An example would be ethnic boundaries which divide or separate ethnic groups on the basis of features including language, dress, religion, or material culture. Physical or territorial boundaries, on the other hand, have some basis in the natural world, such as rivers, differing elevation or climate, or a human-made line or barrier. Physical and social barriers may coincide, but in many cases they do not (e.g., Bonzani 1992:211–212).

A final distinction worth noting is between "artificial" and "natural" boundaries. Although it is my contention here that all boundaries are artificial in the sense that they are imposed by human beings, sometimes fairly arbitrarily, on an environment, people have held over time a belief in the existence of natural boundaries, i.e., those which closely conform to some aspect of the natural environment (Peattie 1944:53–54). The idea of natural boundaries has been powerful force at certain times and in certain cultures, e.g., as part of French national policy (Hartshorne 1936:57; Fischer 1949:199–200; Sahlins 1989, 1990; Carlisle 1996:37–38).

Boundaries, like borders and frontiers, are one of the ways in which human beings impose a spatial structure, an order, on their environment. In this sense boundaries are necessarily social constructions (Kristof 1959; Carlisle 1996:39; Pellow 1996:2). As human constructs, the functions and conceptions of boundaries have evolved as cultural and sociopolitical complexity and organization has increased. Although tribal boundaries tend to be less well defined, more diffuse and permeable than those of more complex societies, under given circumstances they can be carefully demarcated and rigidly maintained (Hodder 1982; Thornton 1982). However, the origin of the state significantly changed the nature and importance of boundaries, partly as a response to the increasing value of land and the accompanying increase in territoriality. As the importance of territory increased and as greater need to restrict mobility across borders emerged, boundaries became increasingly more significant and much greater attention was paid to their location, definition and maintenance (Fischer 1949:217; Kratochwil 1986). And, as we shall see, the development of the state also created and strongly influenced other aspects of spatial organization, including borders and frontiers.

Borders

As part of the effort to understand the meaning of the next concept, of borders or borderlands, it is necessary initially to distinguish the border from the frontier. As will become apparent, although they are often used interchangeably or synonymously (sometimes within the same sentence or paragraph), much more discussion has been devoted to the meaning and nature of frontiers. For purposes of clarity, I propose to define the border as that area of a sedentary society extending from the boundary of its core zone to the limits of its effective political control (Figure 1); the frontier, on the other hand, is that area which lies beyond the outer limit or boundary of the border zone (Feuer 1983:14; cf. Edmonds 1985:19; Adelman and Aron 1999:815–816; Haefeli 1999).

1. Boundaries, Borders and Frontiers

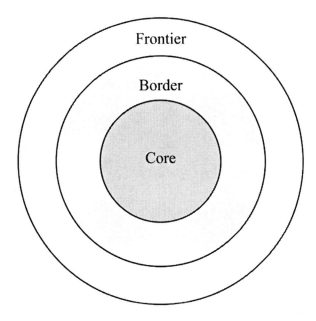

Figure 1: Schematic Model of Core/Border/Frontier

In terms of the spatial models referred to earlier, border zones are conceived as less fully integrated than the core zone and are often perceived as less sophisticated, less developed and more provincial than the center or core; in world-systems terminology a border is equivalent to a semi-periphery (Wallerstein 1974:349–350; Wilkinson 1991:151; Hall 2000:252). According to Chase-Dunn and Hall a semi-periphery is located between core and peripheral regions, mixes forms of both core and peripheral organization, involves mediating activities between core and periphery, and contains intermediate institutional features (Figure 2). Moreover, because of their intermediate position, border zones are especially fertile venues for social innovation and change (1991:21, 30).

In order for a border to exist, there must be sufficient internal differentiation within a society and some differential development and organization to comprise a center and periphery. Consequently, where two states border each other, the boundary between them divides the border of one state from that of the other (cf. Edmonds 1985:19). As states expand and develop, what may have begun as a

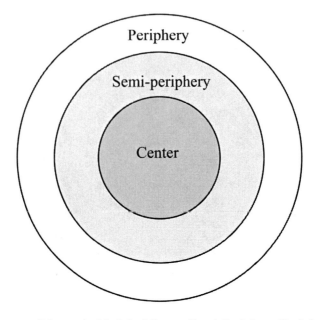

Figure 2: Schematic Model of Center/Semi-Periphery/Periphery

diffuse peripheral zone typically narrows until a distinct boundary is defined.

Frontiers

Although frontiers have presumably existed from the beginning of human prehistory, the conceptualization of, references to, and words for frontiers date to the earliest empires (e.g., Edmonds 1985:19). The Romans used *limes, front* and *frontis* to refer to peripheral regions, the former evolving into the modern *limit*, while the latter two terms indicate a forward or front area (Forbes 1968:205; Hanson 1989:55; Elton 1996:126). In the 13th century AD, the rulers of France began to use the words *limites* and *frontiers* to formalize a similar distinction between the limits of jurisdiction on the one hand and a further zone where armed encounters with other groups might take place (Sahlins 1990:1425–1426); this distinction, we can see, accords nicely with my earlier differentiation of borders and frontiers. It was only in the 19th century, according to Febvre (1922), that the concepts of the fixed military front and territorial boundary merged (cf. Whittaker 1994:7–8). In addition to confusion among boundaries, borders and frontiers, the meaning of the latter word has different connotations in different languages (e.g., Webb 1952:2–3; Gottmann 1973:134; Weber and Rausch 1994:xiii; Elton 1996:127), and, moreover, some of these meanings have changed over time.

The study of frontiers began formally in the work of the 19th-century American historian Frederick Jackson Turner, whose "frontier hypothesis" concerned, *inter alia*, the impact of the frontier on American culture and society. However, it later became apparent that his characterization of the frontier was limited in its application to other frontier situations. This realization led in turn to scholars formulating many definitions of the frontier, often overlapping in their primary elements, each focusing on or emphasizing particular aspects. I include several here not necessarily to indicate a preference for one over another, but rather to indicate some of the most significant features which might contribute to a firmer understanding of these primary elements. Here are three extended definitions of the frontier:

> 1. A frontier may be defined as a region in which the dispersal of settlement into a new territory takes place. It is the zone that separates the unsettled and settled portions of a territory that lie within or under the effective control of a state. Collectively it is referred to as the area of colonization. As a temporal phenomenon, the frontier arises with the first influx of permanent settlement and ceases to exist only when an upper limit of growth is achieved, accompanied by a stabilization of the settlement pattern.
>
> Thus, the frontier may also be seen as a geographical expression of an exchange network designed to permit the incorporation of unsettled territory into a larger socioeconomic system. Frontier settlements function as nodes in this network and reflect the distribution of personnel and materials in the most efficient way to permit the integration of activities in a sparsely settled area. The limits of the exchange network at any given time effectively mark the boundaries of the area of colonization [Lewis 1977:154].
>
> 2. A frontier is an area of interpenetration between societies. It contains three elements: a territorial element, a zone or territory as distinct from a boundary line; a human element, comprising peoples of initially separate and distinct societies; and the process by which relations

among such peoples commence, develop, and eventually crystallize. A frontier opens with the first contact between the members of two societies. It closes when a single authority has established political and economic hegemony over the zone. When we talk of a frontier closing, we do not imply that the relations between the inhabitants become static or rigid, but rather that a new structural situation has been created and the ongoing historical process is no longer a frontier process [Thompson 1983:102].

3. A frontier system is a dynamic social network of a particular kind which covers an extensive geographic area and which links a number of culturally diverse societies; a frontier system is distinguished by the presence of four characteristics: (1) one or more foci; (2) territorial expansion of people from the focus; (3) direct contact by the expanding people with culturally distinct societies; (4) the presence of a single communication network which links the various societies of the frontier system together; a frontier society is any society within a frontier system; the dynamic nature of the frontier system is a consequence of continuous, structured change which occurs throughout the system [Wells 1973:6].

Looking at some of the common threads in these definitions, we can extract the following key elements common to frontiers: (1) a region into which a society expands, or colonizes, usually occupied by another culture at a lower level of social, cultural and economic development (if both societies are at a similar level of development, it would be a border, not a frontier, as discussed earlier); (2) an area where two or more groups interact in various ways; (3) an area beyond the sphere of state control (Kopytoff 1987:28); (4) a network of social, political and economic communication connecting the core to the periphery and the periphery to further regions (cf. Thompson and Lamar 1981:8). Moreover, by definition, a frontier cannot exist without a previously established core area or center, implying a structural linkage between a concept of frontier and a concept of heartland, core or key area (Riley 1982:1; Nelson 1993:175). As noted previously, frontiers contain "persons and territories beyond the effective formal or official political-religious control of the home society and as places where personal lifestyles differ significantly from those of the heartland" (Helms 1988:50). Those attracted to the frontier and seeking sanctuary included debtors, lawbreakers, those fleeing unhappy marriages (Owsley 1945:147), and "in general, frontiers attract the restless and adventurous" (Hennessey 1978:110), those people or groups less satisfied with or committed to the *status quo*.

Kinds of Frontiers

Since spatial phenomena can be studied at a number of different levels, as I noted in my earlier discussion of boundaries, it is possible to construct a taxonomy of frontiers. Such a classificatory scheme, such as that proposed by Thompson and Lamar, would encompass, at the highest level of abstraction, the frontier process as a general human experience in space and time, an intermediate level concerning world systems in a particular place at a particular time, a lower level comprising regional divisions of imperial frontiers, and the lowest level involving smaller areas and communities (1981:11; cf. Thompson 1983:103). I am, of course, dealing with the highest level in this introduction, but will be referring to lower levels—most specifically Mycenaean Thessaly—as illustrations of the aspects discussed here.

As the result of the comparative frontier studies discussed above, various kinds of frontiers have been described, discussed, compared and analyzed. Some of the most significant variables leading to different types of frontiers include the amount of technological differentiation between societies, the occupations of participants in a frontier zone, and the extent of commitment of each of the interacting societies (Thompson 1983:102; Weber and Rausch 1994:xxiii). Here I wish, in order to indicate the range of frontier situations and possibilities, to consider briefly some of the most significant kinds of frontiers. One distinction commonly made, for example, contrasts open or dynamic frontiers, which are in the process of growth and expansion, with closed or static frontiers, which have ceased their external growth and have either stabilized or have focused more on internal development; the ultimate result of this frontier process is often the transformation of a frontier into a border (Lattimore 1962; Lewis 1977:154; Thompson and Lamar 1981:7; Willems 1983:106; Winks 1983:141; Whittaker 1994:5–7).

Another distinction, based primarily on social and economic needs and values, is that between frontiers of inclusion, wherein the indigenous population was valued primarily as a labor source or as a target of religious conversion, and frontiers of exclusion, wherein the natives were excluded on religious, racial or ethnic grounds (Lattimore 1962; Hennessy 1978:19). In terms of some of the kinds of inter-

19

actions to be discussed subsequently, this might involve a contrast between efforts at assimilation on the one hand or extermination on the other (Mikesell 1968; Weber 1986:71–72). Frontiers of inclusion and exclusion are also similar to open and closed frontiers (Willems 1983:106).

Yet another related distinction is that between external and internal frontiers or colonies (Lewis 1958:480–481; Kopytoff 1987:14, 27; Triulzi 1994:235, 238; Whittaker 1994:129). To some extent the idea of the internal frontier or colony overlaps with that of a border region in the sense that it lies within state jurisdictional boundaries rather than outside them. Also, therefore, external frontiers may evolve into internal ones as the territory and boundaries of the state expand, thus often modifying the function of the area as well: "A group that lives on an external frontier is more likely to serve as a buffer than a barrier. In contrast, an *internal frontier* is encapsulated within an expanding system" (Hall 2000:251). Hall also notes that over time internal frontiers become more common than external ones (2000:260).

One type of frontier which became widespread and prominent— and therefore has been studied intensively—is colonies. Colonies may be considered a kind of discontinuous frontier, since they are by definition separated from the homeland or core area by some form of natural barrier, usually water. According to Tartaron (2005:153; cf. Branigan 1981:25; Gosden 2004:2–3; Stein 2005:10–11):

> A colony may be defined as an intrusive settlement established for long-term residence by one society in uninhabited territory or in the territory of another society. In the latter case, the colony is at least at the outset spatially and socially separate from the host community, and possesses a distinct corporate identity expressed culturally, economically, and/or politically, though the cultural distinctiveness may erode over time. Colonies may be established for a variety of purposes: to facilitate trade, to establish defensive networks, to relieve demographic or resource pressure, etc.

Various kinds of colonies have been identified, described and discussed, including governed colonies, settlement colonies, community colonies (Branigan 1981, 1984; cf. Schofield 1984), and extractive colonies (Pailes and Reff 1985). Other functions of colonies in addition to trade and resource extraction include military or administrative out-

1. Boundaries, Borders and Frontiers

posts and places of refuge (Stein 2005:11). The process by which frontiers are settled and inhabited is often referred to as colonization, and thus the frontier may be considered an area of colonization (Lewis 1977:154; Wells 1973:7; Green 1979:70–71). Since states and empires are usually the agents of colonization, there is often some relationship between colonialism and imperialism, although this is not necessarily always the case (Okun 1989:12; Stein 2005:12). But as Bartel observes, "the critical difference between colonialism and imperialism is the presence or absence of significant numbers of permanent settlers in the colony from the colonizing power.... Critical is the amount of civilian composition from the colonizing power; if only military presence resides within a colony it may be thought of as more an imperialist strategy" (1980:15).

As peripheral zones, both borders and frontiers function as transitional areas, often characterized as buffer zones or no man's lands. Sometimes these regions are uninhabited or virtually so, representing areas not entirely under the control of, or indirectly controlled by, the societies bordering them, i.e., neutral or liminal zones which are marginal in terms of utilization by any particular group (Price 1973:2; Kratochwil 1984:40; Cherry 1987:155–156; Bonzani 1992). For tribal or chiefdom-level societies such wild lands might be used for hunting or pasturage, although these activities might be challenged by other groups (Hickerson 1965; DeBoer 1981; De Atley 1984:5; Gibson 1988:46; Larsson 1988:100–103). For states or empires buffer zones served as the first line of defense, a protective barrier to any assault or invasion of the core region as well as an intermediate zone in terms of economic activities and transactions (Eadie 1977:231; Hedeager 1979; Braund 1984; Haselgrove 1984:35–36; Kopytoff 1987:28–29; Cunliffe 1988:184; Champion 1989:6; Okey 1992:105; Hall 2000:252). Such regions thus act as a kind of filter of the movement and transmission of energy, information, people and objects (Bonzani 1992:212).

Because two or more groups encounter each other regularly in peripheral zones and because political and economic control there, at least in preindustrial times (pace Wallerstein et al.) are more tenuous, border and frontier areas are almost by definition liminal zones, indeterminate space wherein interaction and change can occur more readily than elsewhere. Within this contact zone (Whitney 1970; Wells 1973:10; Edmonds 1985:21; Pratt 1992: Blake 1999) a condition of indeterminacy exists which has been variously characterized as a third space (Bhabha 1996, 2004; Graner and Karlanby 2007:150; Varberg 2007:61–62), middle ground (White 1991; Malkin 2002:151–153; Hodos 2006) or contested ground (Guy and Sheridan 1998; Hall 1998, 2000:241).

The idea of third space derives from an analysis of recent colonial situations. According to Homi Bhabha, a third space exists between the extremes of colonizer and colonized which is a theater of communication and negotiation, an in-between space wherein cultural hybridity is created as a result of the ambivalence of the actors and their ambiguity of their relationship (2004; Antonaccio 2003:59–60; cf. van Dommelen 2005, 2006; Wu 2013).

Middle ground, a concept originated by Richard White, "is the place in between: in between cultures, peoples, and in between empires and the nonstate world of villages" (1991:x). Middle ground is by definition territory—whether physical or social—in which the potential for accommodation exists because neither group is able, for various reasons, to impose their will upon the other (White 1991:x). Since unilateral domination—as the traditional colonial model stipulates—is not possible under these circumstances, the middle ground is also both core and periphery in terms of influence (Hodos 2006:86; 2009:222; Tsetskhladze 2006:lvi). Given the inability of both sides to gain their ends through force, emphasis shifts toward cooperation, achieving common understanding and the creation of a culture based upon mutual invention (White 1991:50–52).

Thus the focus of middle ground interaction is on the role of mutual need and accommodation (Hodos 2006, 2009:221) resulting in the transformation of both groups (Gosden 2004), often resulting in hybrid cultures through a process White (1991:x) describes as a kind of creative and often expedient misunderstanding. One of the central and defining aspects of a middle ground is the willingness of those who created it to justify their own actions in terms of what they perceive to be their partner's cultural premises; while those operating in the middle ground may have acted for interests derived from their own culture, they had to convince people of another culture that some mutual action was fair and legitimate (Hodos 2006:155–156).

Arguing that most ancient empires and colonies resulted from "a combination of middle ground and control of networks within a shared cultural milieu," Gosden (2004:40) describes the middle ground as an arena of creativity and tension, a destabilizing environment which opens possibilities for a transformation of values. He also notes that a middle ground cannot occur if either party is considered the Other (2004:105).

Although each of these concepts is slightly different, they overlap in sharing the notion of open-ended possibilities whereby the inhabitants of these regions have the opportunity to negotiate an identity through the agency of choice (Dietler 1997; Woolf 1998; Sherratt 1999; Antonaccio 2003:60; Broodbank 2004). One useful concept here is that of negotiated peripherality, whereby groups or individuals in peripheral zones were sometimes able to structure or determine their relationships with larger, more complex, and more powerful societies (Kardulias 1999, 2002; Schon and Galaty 2006; cf. Tartaron 2005).

As should now be apparent, many different kinds of boundaries and frontiers have been proposed. This suggests that not only are these terms broadly conceived and applied, but that both frontiers and boundaries can be classified in various ways. One reason for this variety is that certain variables influence the nature of peripheral zones; two of the most significant sets of variables involve geographical factors on the one hand and the degree or nature of sociocultural complexity on the other (Hennessey 1978:6). Not only has our conception of frontiers and borders changed and been modified as the result of previous research, but as already indicated, boundaries, borders and frontiers are dynamic and themselves evolve over time. Beginning with the creation of a frontier by the entry of groups or individuals into previously unknown territory, their extent and nature evolve according to a congeries of variables (Thompson and Lamar 1981:9–10).

2

Theoretical and Methodological Issues

Having identified and discussed the key concepts concerning spatial variability, I will now examine in some detail the theoretical constructs and methodological implications which underlie these concepts, particularly in respect to past human behavior. The two basic theories I consider here are those of the archaeological culture and the center/periphery relationship.

It is difficult, if not impossible, to make meaningful inferences about the past without being able to identify or use analytical units which convey some understanding of the manner in which human beings group themselves and function as cultural entities. There are, it seems to me, two not entirely incompatible approaches to this problem. One is to work backward from a more clearly understood and more easily accessible knowledge of the present and recent past, a method often referred to as ethnographic analogy or direct historical record (cf. Chang and Tourtellotte 1993:254). Another is to infer groupings in the archaeological record from the distribution of material culture.

Before discussing the archaeological culture concept, therefore, let me briefly articulate some of the theoretical grounds and methodological issues concerning the relationship of past and present in respect to human behavior. One underlying assumption is that some human behavior is relatively invariable and has not changed or evolved appreciably over time. And although we will see that other aspects of human activity regarding the perception and partitioning of space did evolve (Chapter 4), making this assumption enables the comparison of different time periods. Clearly such an understanding or belief would be useful in attempting to compare modern observable behavior or historically attested behavior with an archaeological record in which such evidence does not exist or is more difficult to interpret. Of course, all interpretation of archaeological data is to some extent inferential, so here I am merely making explicit one basis for making such inferences.

Generally the most fully understood and completely documented human activity is that which can be accessed in the present or the recent past. Typically, therefore, the more one delves into the past, the less complete, less accurate and less accessible is the record of human behavior. One can, however, construct a chain of evidence and inference connecting increasingly less reliable source material based upon homologies or similarities in different time periods, utilizing respectively contemporary, ethnographic, ethnohistoric, ethnoarchaeological, historical, and archaeological contexts. Each of these contexts demonstrates some continuity and isomorphism with the others, but also differs in significant ways as well.

As should already be evident, I have drawn upon all of these sources of evidence and time periods in my discussion of basic concepts, and it should also be evident that the clearest and fullest expression and illustration of those concepts can be found in contemporary contexts. This relationship between past and present will be crucial as well in discussing the evolution of spatial concepts and behavior (Chapter 3) and the case studies which conclude the book (Chapter 5).

Archaeological Cultures

The concept of archaeological cultures arose in the nineteenth century as the discipline of archaeology began to adopt a more scientific approach to studying the prehistoric past. This concept originated in an effort to organize the material remains of European Neolithic and Bronze Age tribal cultures which were (wrongly) assumed to be relatively simple sedentary and internally homogenous entities with sharply demarcated boundaries (Trigger 1977:22). In addition to recognizing past societies known from legend, tradition, oral history, and written history based upon the analysis of material remains, previously unknown cultures were also identified on the basis of unique assemblages of artifacts. The initial approach, most fully articulated by the German prehistorian Kossinna, was straightforward: past cultures could be identified and characterized by a unique assemblage; there was thus a one-to-one relationship between a people and a distinctive set of artifacts. This concept was subsequently elaborated by Childe and others:

> One of the principal assumptions underlying the culture-historical approach is that bounded, homogeneous cultural entities correlate with particular peoples, ethnic groups, tribes, and/or races. The assumption was based on a normative conception of culture, that within a given group cultural practices and beliefs tend to conform to prescriptive ideational norms or rules of behavior [Jones 1997:24; cf. Renfrew 1978:92; Hodder 1982:2–8; Shennan 1989:5–11; Diaz-Andreu and Lucy 2005:2; Raymond 2005:180].

Considerable effort was expended in defining an ideal culture-unit (Naroll 1964), of which the archaeological culture represented an extension into the past, but it proved to be a difficult idea to operationalize (Brown 1984:429; Jones 1997:50–52). The use of trait lists, for example, to isolate cultural groups assumed that territorial contiguity, ecological adaptation or linguistic affiliation would reflect a cultural reality, but such assumptions were not supported by ethnographic data, let alone archaeological evidence (Kamp and Yoffee 1980:94–95). It became clear that sharply defined and unambiguous cultural boundaries were the exception rather than the rule and that there was usually some overlap in the distribution of traits, whether individual or grouped.

This led David Clarke to propose a polythetic approach to the differing distributions of artifacts which comprise a recurrent assemblage, whereby "a polythetic group is a group of entities such that each entity possesses a large number of the attributes of the group, each attribute is shared by large numbers of entities and no single attribute is both sufficient and necessary to the group membership" (1978:36; cf. Renfrew 1978:92; Hodder 1982:2–7; Urban and Schortman 1988:252; Shennan 1989:42–47). Although the polythetic approach more closely reflected the more complex interconnection and overlapping of social, cultural, ethnic, linguistic and political identities and associations, it also, needless to say, complicated the analysis of such entities.

Even so, both the reality and the usefulness of archaeological cultures have been questioned. Trigger, for example, wonders whether the concept of the archaeological culture is appropriate for analysis of hunter/gatherers or early civilizations (1984:283). And as Chernela also asserts, the conflation or presumed isomorphism of social and spatial distance or social and physical proximity is an idea which in fact cannot and should not necessarily be assumed (1992:111; cf. Stone 1992:152–153; Day et al. 1998:140).

Thus the concept of the archaeological culture has both evolved and been widely criticized, but it seems difficult to discuss many aspects of past human behavior, particularly those with a spatial dimension, without some basic unit of analysis. Therefore, although there are certainly limitations on the kinds of inferences that can be made, I nonetheless accept the concept as a starting point in attempting to understand past human spatial organization and behavior, agreeing with Shennan that an archaeological culture "is thus to be understood as a term for an entity which is spatially and chronologically distinguishable within the general cultural development" (1989:46).

Spatial Models

The meaning and significance of archaeological cultures becomes evident when we turn our attention to the dominant theoretical construct of center and periphery, since identifying and characterizing these constituent elements in the archaeological record necessitates the use of archaeological cultures or their equivalent. One influential model, "virtually a theoretical archetype" (Randsborg 1992:8; cf. Bilde 1993:9) which has been utilized extensively and which has been widely used in particular by Immanuel Wallerstein (1974; cf. Galtung 1972) and subsequent world-systems analysts (Chase-Dunn and Hall 1991; Wilkinson 1991:121; Sanderson 1995; Hall 2000:238; cf. Santley and Alexander 1989:47) is that of core/center and periphery, based on the assumption that people structure space in terms of a central or core area surrounded or bordered by one or more peripheral or marginal zones (Shils 1975:3; Cherry 1987:164; Mellor 1989:58). According to Fernandez "the centre/periphery phenomenon is perpetual in human experience, if only because it is an inevitable projection of crucial corporeal experiences of vital centres of the body and useful but less vital appendages, a corporeal experience which is then projected into spatial concomitants of greater or lesser vitality—or greater or lesser power" (2000:118).

An underlying assumption not always explicitly stated is that the core or center is considered more significant or important than the periphery. Moreover, "there is some agreement that the centre-periphery metaphor, as used in the social sciences, entails two assumptions: (1) that the centre is the locus of decision-making, i.e., of power; (2) that they both belong to an encompassing system, of which they are differentiated but interdependent parts" (Strassoldo 1980:37–38; cf. Gottman 1980:17; Wilkinson 1991:122; Bilde 1993:9).

> The concepts of centre and periphery, in various ways and in various degrees of specificity, have had a long history in western European thought. Such opposed ideas as town and country, civilized and barbarian, long engrained in our thinking, implicitly embody them. The western construction of history, with its emphasis on the rise and fall of the classical world, the emergence of its north and west European successor states and their rise to world dominance, also incorporates a contrast between an innovative, developing, dynamic and dominant region and others which are backward and ultimately subjected. This contrast is both a spatial one, with the dynamic region of western Europe surrounded on all sides by less developed territories, and a cultural one, defining western Europe as an area of particular interest and values, to be studied, appreciated and maintained in a way very different from the regions beyond [Champion 1989:2; cf. Strassoldo 1980:52; Wolf 1982; Randsborg 1992:8; Bilde 1993:9; Whittaker 1994:17].

Beyond identifying, differentiating and characterizing different spatial zones, the center/periphery model also concerns the dynamic relationship between core and periphery, particularly in terms of the linkages between them (Cohen and Maier 1983:293; Lerner 1987:98; Ucko 1989:xv); by establishing such linkages, the core in fact creates the periphery by engaging other regions within a broader exchange system, thus making them economically and politically dependent (Stein 1998:224). One of Wallerstein's contributions to such analyses was the idea that relationships between societies could also be a primary determinant of social change within societies (Shipley 1993:212). It also is important to understand, however, that the core/periphery model does not solely concern spatial relationships, but economic, political and social interrelationships as well (Randsborg 1992:8; Bilde

2. Theoretical and Methodological Issues

1993:9; cf. Whitecotton and Pailes 1986:194). It is, in addition, "as much a matter of attitude and perception as it is of fact and physical location" (Ucko 1989:xv).

Although Wallerstein's initial model was relatively simple and straightforward—particularly as it applied to modern Western capitalism—subsequent analysis and discussion has simultaneously broadened and refined the original model to apply to a much wider variety of levels encompassed within the world-system concept (e.g., Cunliffe 1988:3; Lightfoot and Martinez 1995:477), as well as variation in the structure of many existing and possible core-periphery systems and the nature of articulation and interaction between core and periphery (Santley and Alexander 1989:31: Ucko 1989:xv; Hall 1991:213; Rice 1998:45–7). Not only are relationships between core and periphery dominated by economic exchanges administered under a variety of political systems (Cunliffe 1988:3), but also by different levels of socio/political/cultural organization in both the center and the periphery—although the level of organization is always greater in the center (Lerner 1987:97). From an economic perspective—which is the primary emphasis of the model—the world system is

> a macroregional division of labor linking culturally diverse polities and leading to wealth and power differentials between core and periphery. The core is a center of accumulation, heightened consumption, specialized manufacturing, political power, and (sometimes) rigid political integration. The periphery is made up of producers of raw materials who become increasingly specialized (and therefore unstable) through time. A world system is founded on unbalanced exchange, which drains resources from the peripheries and amasses them at the core. The main beneficiaries are a small group of elites, located in both core and periphery, who jointly dominate the system [Nelson 1993:76; cf. Strassoldo 1980:42–43; Thompson and Lamar 1981:9; Wolf 1982; Cherry 1987:167].

As noted, although Wallerstein claimed considerable scope for a model characterizing modern Western capitalism, the model was soon applied to a much wider variety of contexts and, not surprisingly, was found to be insufficient or inadequate in a number of respects (Woolf 1990:45; Rice 1998:46; Stein 1998:225–228). One frequent criticism of this model was that it propounded a largely diffusionist colonial perspective whereby the center was perceived as active, directive and dominant, while the periphery was portrayed as mere extensions of the center which were passive, receptive, culturally marginal and backward, with a focus on dependency rather than autonomous development (McGuire 1986:245; Lerner 1987:97; Schortman and Urban 1987:55–56; Wright 1987:61–62; Lightfoot and Martinez 1995:475–477; Rice 1998:46). There is no reason, however, why the model needs to be deterministic in this way, and there can be potentially a range of outcomes or trajectories over time, including the emergence of a new center in a former periphery (e.g., Paynter 1981:119–121; Bloemers 1989:177).

In summary,

> the world system model rests on three fundamental, but problematic, assumptions.... First, it assumes a fundamental power asymmetry between the different parts of the system so that the core politically dominated the periphery, either through direct colonial administration or through a combination of economic and cultural hegemony. Second, the model assumes that as a result of these asymmetries the core was able to control the exchange system. Third, the model assumes that long-distance exchange relations structure all other aspects of political economy in peripheral societies [Stein 1998:225–226].

Another significant area where the core/periphery model was found to be inadequate or largely inapplicable and therefore requiring modification was in pre-modern or prehistoric contexts. Schortman and Urban draw attention to the primarily economic orientation of Wallerstein's model, more appropriate for the modern world system, and a consequent lack of attention to the social systems with which anthropologists and archaeologists are traditionally concerned (1987:58; Ragin and Chirot 1984; Kohl 1987:59). Champion also points out that Wallerstein's model dichotomizes social systems into small-scale subsistence economies on the one hand and world systems on the other and thus ignores many other types of socioeconomic arrangements that fall in between (1989:7). Many archaeologists have also noted that pre-modern societies, even those such as ancient Greece and Rome which were colonial or imperial polities, did not conform to the Western capitalist world-system, due in part to differing economic, political and social structures.

Kohl, most notably, observed that the world systems of antiquity probably only superficially resembled those of modern times, suggesting that the rankings of cores and peripheries were probably less stable

2. Theoretical and Methodological Issues

than they are now and that political force may have played a more overt role in regulating them (1987, 1989; cf. Paynter 1981; Trigger 1984:286; Schortman and Urban 1987:57–63; Champion 1989; Santley and Alexander 1989; Shipley 1993; Stein 1998:226–7).

Specifically, for Bronze Age societies of the Old World at least three features distinguish ancient world systems from that of the modern era: (1) the nature of ancient empires and the extent of economic dependency created between imperial powers and their colonies; (2) the multiplicity of noncontiguous, politically and economically independent but contemporaneous and overlapping mini-world systems in antiquity, a feature resulting in relatively loose ties of dependency between cores and peripheries; and (3) the possibility—even probability at certain times and in certain spheres, such as metal-working and horse-breeding—of technological parity and superiority of peripheries over core states (Kohl 1992:118).

Likewise, Speilmann believes that most aspects of the core/periphery model are not applicable to non-hierarchical societies (1991:6–7); Arafat and Morgan deny that the model is appropriate for Classical Greece (1994:32); and Millet (1970:6–7) suggests that simple forms of the model do not apply to the Roman empire either (cf. Horden and Purcell 2000:133). Other criticisms are that Wallerstein tends to minimize the role of luxury items or "preciocities" in trade relationships at the expense of "necessities" or basic goods, and that the model pays insufficient attention to variability in local or regional economies and how local economies might affect or influence regional political or economic structures (Rice 1998:46).

Although much of the initial work of world-systems theorists focused on the core or center and its relationship with the periphery, and was therefore less suitable for frontier studies (Edmonds 1985:20), more recent analyses have shifted emphasis to the periphery and adopted a perspective from the border or frontier rather than the core (Lightfoot and Martinez 1995; Lerner 1987:103; Rice 1998:45–47; Wright 1987:66). Hall, for example, proposes to develop a "world-systems analysis of frontiers" (2000:238), and that is obviously similar to the approach that I am taking here as well. Thus despite the limitations of Wallerstein's modern world systems model discussed above, and though some believe that "world systems theory, despite its title, is more a description than a theory" (Gosden 2004:17), the core/periphery model retains considerable utility for the study of borders and frontiers. There is no question, for example, that most, if not all, human groups perceive the space they inhabit as comprising central and peripheral areas, or that there is a relationship between them.

A second, related model views the spatial distribution of groups or cultures in terms of greater or lesser integration or control (Braudel 1972:355; Cherry 1987:155–156, 165). This model is not by any means incompatible with the core/periphery model since one of its premises is that various forms of organization—cultural, political, social, economic—are more highly integrated in the center or core and less so on the periphery (Shils 1975:70). An additional premise is that there are various relationships between the more highly integrated center and the less-integrated periphery. Idealized forms of both models either explicitly indicate or imply successive and widening concentric circles (Figure 3), but realities on the ground inevitably distort such an idealized picture (e.g., Helms 1988:31; Sinopoli 1994:169). A variant of concentric circles is the incomplete wheel model proposed by Motyl (2001:16–19).

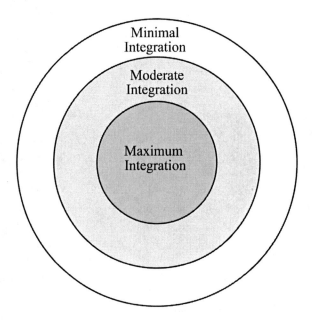

Minimal
Integration

Moderate
Integration

Maximum
Integration

Figure 3: Schematic Model of Increasing/Decreasing Integration

2. Theoretical and Methodological Issues

Integration may be defined as interdependence or interconnect-edness between parts whereby interdependence represents the total amount of flow of matter, energy or information between system components; centralization is a highly developed form of integration (Kowalewski et al. 1983:35), but a system can be strongly integrated yet relatively decentralized if, for example, parts of the periphery are more closely connected to each other than to the core or center. Clearly, integration is variable within a system, depending upon which subsystem is involved and the degree to which individual and groups participate and are included in various processes and activities. Even in the simplest societies, for example, there is differential participation according to basic variables such as age and gender, and this differential participation is considerably greater in hierarchically structured societies, in terms, e.g., of integration into political, economic, social, cultural and religious activities (Linton 1936; Binford 1965; Burger 1984:41; Feuer 1999).

In larger and more complex societies, this kind of differential integration begins to have a spatial dimension as well, whereby the periphery is by definition less well integrated into a sociocultural system than the center. This is to say that although there is differential integration even within the core, integration tends to become attenuated over distance (cf. Stein 1998:225–226). Thus, although an idealized pattern of increasing and/or decreasing integration is complicated by the fact that some groups and individuals in the periphery, such as local elites, may be more strongly integrated into the system than lower-ranking or more marginal individuals or groups in the center, one may conceive of this phenomenon in a general way of zones of increasing or decreasing integration (e.g., Lattimore 1962; Groenman-van Wateringe 1980; De Atley 1984; Kopytoff 1987:29). It can be seen, again, that such a conception is essentially similar to that of center, semi-periphery and periphery (cf. Schortman and Urban 1987:58).

It is impossible for any society to be fully integrated. It is also impossible for it to be completely unintegrated.... Ecologically, too, as the distance from the center increases, there is a diminution in the effectiveness of integration of all types. Those parts of the society which are in more attenuated intercourse with the center are likely to be less integrated culturally into the center and more recalcitrant toward efforts to bring them under the authority of the center.... The degree of directness of integration likewise varies among societies and from one part of society to another. Some parts are integrated to the center of society through a "link." Leaders of groups which are integrated are often more integrated than their followers who might be integrated primarily to them and then through them to the center.... Integration is not homogeneous over the entire society. It is never more than partial. It is not constant or continuous. It is frequently shifting from one part of society to others. In some respects, various parts of the society might be well integrated, others less so; on other issues, the integratedness might have quite a different structure [Shils 1975:80–81].

Integration may be achieved in various respects—i.e., economic, political, social, cultural, religious. etc.—and there is no necessary reason why the degree or intensity of integration should be similar in different arenas of human activity; in fact, given the nature of the societies involved in core and periphery, there are often good reasons why integration is demanded or resisted in one area and not in another. It is often the case, for example, in colonial situations that economic integration is encouraged or enforced while other forms of integration are discouraged or less emphasized. Chapman (1990:115–116) identifies three forces of integration—identitive, utilitarian and coercive—operating on two levels of society, elites and the masses; identitive bonds are recognized as communal symbols such as language, religion and ethnicity, while utilitarian bonds tend to focus on economic self-interest. I will discuss such integrative processes subsequently (Chapter 4), but here will only specify them broadly as including *inter alia* trade, diffusion, articulation, incorporation, acculturation, syncretism and assimilation (e.g., Roymans 1983; van der Leeuw 1983; Bloemers 1991).

A similar approach can be discerned in the distance-parity model, based upon the assumption that the ability of the center to exert control and power decays or declines with distance, thus leading to increasing parity between core and periphery as distance increases. As a result of relatively limited interaction between center and periphery, the periphery does not necessarily become economically dependent on the core. "Economic compartmentalization and the lack of fungibility or interchangeability between different spheres of economic activity would tend to limit the degree to which small-scale elite exchanges of luxury goods could have transformed entire economic systems in the periphery" (Stein 1998:229; cf. Kohl 1987, 1989). According to this model, variability of interregional exchange systems is structured by one or more of the following: the balance of power between polities; the effects of distance on transport costs; differential regional access to technology; and demographic and ecological conditions.

Another related and somewhat complementary model which also emphasizes large-scale sociocultural interaction is peer polity interaction (Renfrew and Cherry 1986; cf. Champion 1989:9–10), which focuses on change stimulated by elite emulative competition and thus highlights exogenous change rather than the endogenously-oriented explanation of change of the world systems model. Yet another alternative model envisions the dynamic interpenetration of cultures as overlapping sets, with borders or frontiers as a nexus of integration and competition (Wright 1987:62).

Methodological Issues

Having discussed the primary theoretical approaches to boundaries, borders and frontiers, I now turn my attention to models with a more restricted focus than those discussed above. I divide these into two groups: those concerned with boundaries and those dealing with borders and frontiers.

The most ambitious and comprehensive effort to construct a "general theory of boundaries" was offered by Strassoldo (1977, 1980:45–52; Kristof 1959; Rice 1998:49; cf. Kunstadter 1967:35), who takes a multidisciplinary systems approach emphasizing the openness of contemporary sociocultural systems. This perspective is compatible with the world systems core/periphery model discussed above and utilizes some, but not all, of the same terminology. In addition to offering a typology of boundary situations, Strassoldo also examines boundaries and the concept of boundaries from a variety of disciplinary perspectives, including those of anthropology, sociology, political science, economics and history.

In addition, there has been some methodological discussion concerning the identification of boundaries in the archaeological record. Again, such discussions are based upon assumptions of the existence of archaeological cultures or past sociocultural systems in that in order to define such entities it becomes necessary to establish their boundaries. Most attempts to discern boundaries in an archaeological context rely on several related assumptions: that patterning in the distribution of artifacts reflects group membership; that artifact distribution also indicates the intensity of interaction within and between groups; that interaction diminishes over distance; and that a decline in the frequency of artifact distribution is one possible indication of a boundary between groups. Yet another assumption underlying all of the others is that boundaries calculated on the basis of artifact distribution correspond in any real sense with the perception of boundaries by the groups themselves, an assumption possible to examine in contemporary ethnographic contexts, but more problematical for past societies (Cohen 2000:20).

One such effort is that of Sampson, who proposed a methodology for detecting the boundaries of social territories by combining distribution maps of distinctive artifact types with distributions of source materials, in this case lithic artifacts of foragers, and eliminating the two most common weaknesses of previous attempts by utilizing systematic survey and ethnographic analogy from nearby cultures (1988:15). Moreover, he asserts that "style theory provides the main vehicle for etching territorial boundaries from the archaeological record" (1988:16).

This focus on style as a means of signaling identity is also shared by Hodder, although earlier work dealt with broader aspects of spatial analysis which emphasized artifact distribution (Hodder and Orton 1976; cf. Clarke 1978); a later paper (Kimes et al. 1982; cf. Sellwood 1984) analyzed tribal boundaries based upon the distribution of coins of precious metal. Subsequently, however, Hodder shifted his attention to ethnoarchaeological research concerning aspects of style in establishing and maintaining tribal boundaries (1979, 1982; cf. Wobst 1977; Buchignani 1982, 1987:20; Wiessner 1989; Lightfoot and Martinez 1995:479).

Thus most of the work that has been done in respect to identifying and characterizing social, cultural or ethnic boundaries in the archaeological record concerns the signaling of difference through aspects of style and has been studied through the analysis of artifact distribution patterns. Of course, the analysis of artifact distributions and the construction of distribution maps predates such efforts considerably, but the methodology involved has become considerably more sophisticated. As discussed previously, however, there are many difficulties in putting such analyses into practice. For one, it is not always possible, even in easily-observable or data-rich ethnographic contexts, to distinguish among cultural, social and ethnic identities and thus to determine which identity is being signaled by a given artifact (Barth 1969; Cohen 1969:112). A more serious difficulty arises when, as is often the case, distributions of artifacts do not coincide (Sopher 1972:324–325; Buchignani 1987:20; Jones 1997:49–52; Kowalewski et al. 1983:34; Lightfoot and Martinez 1995:479).

Somewhat different methods have been proposed for locating political boundaries. Renfrew suggests utilizing geographical central place models, marking the hierarchical distribution of central places to define polities and thereby their boundaries (1978:105–106; Renfrew and Level 1979; cf. Alden 1979; Cherry 1987). Such delineations can only be approximate, but since ancient boundaries were rarely defined as precisely as modern ones (see Chapter 3), a certain degree of indeterminacy is probably more desirable than false precision. It should also probably go without saying that other kinds of boundaries must be equally imprecise and that political boundaries probably coincide less with other kinds of boundaries than do social, cultural or ethnic ones; this is certainly the case in the modern world, as noted above.

Unlike boundaries, a wealth of models has been proposed and applied to border and frontier situations (cf. Rice 1998:53–58). The earliest models were often derived from studies of historical areas of interaction between culturally dissimilar groups with radically different levels of sociopolitical complexity; these have sometimes been characterized as multi-cultural frontier models (Demarest 1988:354; Creamer 1984:359). The earliest—and for a long time the most influential—of these models was Frederick Jackson Turner's frontier model.

It can be said, in fact, that the study of frontiers formally began in the work of the 19th-century American historian Frederick Jackson Turner, whose "frontier hypothesis" proposed that many characteristics of American society could be attributed to the influence of the frontier. In his *The Frontier in American History*, Turner defined the frontier as "the temporary boundary of an expanding society at the edge of substantially free lands" (cited in Alexander 1977:25). Elsewhere, however, he used the term, perhaps deliberately, in various other ways which introduced some degree of ambiguity into his application of the concept (Forbes 1968:203, 206; Hennessey 1978:16; Kolchin 1982:67; Weber 1986:67). In many instances, for example, the frontier was, often simultaneously, a place, a process, state of mind or a condition (Webb 1953; Winks 1983:137; Whittaker 1994).

Following Turner's introduction of his frontier concept, subsequent historians, mainly American, attempted to confirm his hypotheses about the American frontier and to refine and modify many of his ideas (Savage and Thompson 1979; Weber 1986:67). For Turner and his followers, the frontier represented "those areas of Anglo-American penetration which had not yet been fully transformed into a stable and completely civilized form of society" (Forbes 1968:203; cf. Newby 1983). This notion was quite rightly criticized as ethnocentric and specifically Eurocentric, with a one-sided focus on the advance of Euro-American civilization, and with little attention paid to its impact on or the responses of aboriginal native Americans (e.g., Webb 1953; Gerhard 1959:206; Wells 1973:6; Thompson and Lamar 1981:4; Winks 1983:141; Weber and Rausch 1994:xiii; Adelman and Aron 1999).

These issues and others gave rise to the field of comparative frontiers whereby different frontiers were compared and contrasted in order to elicit similarities and differences, create a definition of frontiers universally applicable to all equivalent areas and describe, discuss and analyze processes which occurred within them (Kristof 1959; Forbes 1968:207–208; Wells 1973; Thompson 1983:102; Kopytoff 1987:13–14). It became apparent that the American frontier was different in many ways from other frontiers (e.g., Bannon 1970:5–7; Hennessey 1978:16; Eccles 1983; Kopytoff 1987:10), that devising a rubric that included all possible frontier situations beyond a simple and minimal definition would be very difficult, and that the range of variables influencing the nature of frontiers was so extensive that a classification and analysis of various types and kinds of frontiers was more feasible than shoehorning all of them within a one-size-fits-all category (Thompson 1983:102; Kopytoff 1993:143; Elton 1996:127).

Although not all aspects of Turner's model—such as the role of the frontier in shaping American democracy—were perceived as applying elsewhere, the concept of colonization as a wave of successive incursions, mostly in a linear direction, into empty or unoccupied land, was adopted for other areas as well (Winks 1994:141). The dynamic moving frontier, particularly associated with the introduction of agriculture and sedentary life, was seen as an appropriate characterization of many population movements, beginning with the Neolithicization of Europe

2. Theoretical and Methodological Issues

(Alexander and Mohammed 1982:34; Gregg 1988:3–6) and including the Roman empire and the European colonization of the Americas (Kopytoff 1987:8; Rice 1998:49).

Another influential model, emphasizing economic adaptation to a greater extent, was offered by Owen Lattimore in *Studies in Frontier History* (1962). This "model of economic marginality" (Whittaker 1989:66) proposes that societies preferentially expand into environments which are familiar and similar to those of the core zone, growing the same crops under similar ecological conditions (Groenman-van Waateringe 1980; Whittaker 1994). When, however, different environmental circumstances are encountered, in land that cannot not be exploited in an equivalent manner, expansion slows and such territory cannot be incorporated as permanently and successfully; in other words, the boundary between prime and marginal agricultural land is the boundary between the border and the frontier (cf. Feuer 1983). In addition, the people inhabiting these environments are perceived as marginal, with different beliefs and behavior and ambivalent loyalty (Weber 1982:280).

Another economically and ecologically-oriented model is the least effort subsistence model, which employs the analogy of niche and habitat expansion, and "provides a powerful key for cultural-ecological studies through the examination of the adjusting relationships between colonizing populations and their new and old environments" (Green 1979:70). It shares with the economic marginality model a prediction of settlement location where maximum exploitation of land is possible while minimizing social, demographic, and economic distance between the frontier and other settlements (Green 1979:78). This agricultural colonization creates locational marginality resulting from increased distance of frontier settlements from other settlements and the consequent cost of maintaining necessary social, economic, and demographic networks. Locational marginality in turn exerts pressure to increase population density and the demand for labor created by expansion of frontier agriculture (Green 1979:84–85).

Yet another approach, Hudson's locational model of colonial expansion, posits four categories of frontier dynamics (1977). The first two categories represent situations in which there is no serious opposition to movement into a frontier; the concept of adapted spread envisions the transmission of entire trait complexes by the movement of a single unified group into a similar environment to which they are

39

already preadapted. The environmental conflict category, on the other hand, involves movement into increasingly different environments; although Hudson suggests that a demand for new lands on the margins will create a market for innovations, archaeological and historical evidence does not necessarily support this assertion. The other two categories emphasize group conflict arising from conflicts between social groups occupying the same territory (Rice 1998:54).

Lewis' agricultural colonization model shares some of the same elements. Lewis defines the frontier as an area of colonization in which the dispersal of settlement into new territory takes place, enabling its incorporation into a larger sociocultural system. He further specifies the following conditions which characterize it: 1) maintenance of continual contact between colonists and parent society; 2) a lack or loss of complexity due to separation and isolation from trade and communication; 3) geographically dispersed settlement pattern focused around frontier settlements; 4) continued replication of settlement pattern over time as expansion occurs, while areas of earlier settlement become more integrated into and attached to the core area, leading to the formation of a colonization gradient (Lewis 1977, 1984).

Two recent efforts focus more specifically upon processes occurring within peripheries (see Chapter 4). Parker (2006) offers three related models designed to elucidate borderland dynamics. The first model orders and arranges borders and frontiers along a continuum from static closed borders to open fluid frontiers. The second model, termed the Continuum of Boundary Dynamics, envisions peripheries as composites of overlapping categories or "boundary sets": geographic, political, cultural, economic and demographic; the nature of borders or frontiers can thus be specified in terms of the specific configuration of these categories during a given period of time. The third model, termed a Borderland Matrix, graphically depicts the interaction of the various processes over time.

Parker's third model, the Borderland Matrix, also resembles the cross-cultural interaction model proposed by Green and Costion (2016). This is also a visual model which utilizes a series of concentric circles to illustrate processes of cultural exchange and connectivity in borders and frontiers. The model divides the circle into multiple groups in a periphery or peripheries, using arrows to indicate the direction and intensity of interaction.

3

Evolution of
Spatial Concepts

We have seen that one of the salient characteristics of boundaries, borders and frontiers is that they are dynamic and subject to change. In this chapter I will discuss not only the development of individual and specific boundaries, borders and frontiers, but also the evolution of territoriality and other spatial concepts. After considering general evolutionary aspects of spatial organization, I will examine successive phases of development related to increasing social, political and economic complexity.

In general the evolution of spatial patterning and the evolution of human culture are closely correlated (Soja 1971:32; Renfrew 1978:89), so that territoriality, for example, can be seen *inter alia* as the cognitive mapping of social relationships (Sampson 1988:16). It is possible to identify several long-term trends in this process. One is changing conceptions of land tenure and land use (cf. Dodgshon 1987:36). A second is the coevolution of spatial organization and political society (Soja 1971:11–16); changes in the nature of sovereign power are influenced both by technological developments which loosened the bond between people and land and increased the mobility of both people and goods (Gottmann 1973:33). A third and related trend is toward more structured relationships between people and land, resulting in more precise definition of boundaries and between territories (Gottmann 1973:138).

Soja (1971:33) reminds us that

in the long history of human cultural evolution, there have been very few societies which revolved primarily around relatively fixed and clearly defined territorial units. Most frequently, the organization of space was a reflection of internal social and economic structure, and

41

group membership depended less directly upon one's physical location than upon one's position with the social system. These socially defined "boundaries" performed much the same function with respect to trespass, exclusion, and identity as they would have had they been directly expressed or institutionalized on the landscape, but the space they bounded did not necessarily conform to the Euclidean properties of earth space....

Since territoriality is a feature of most animal as well as human populations, one question that arises concerns differences between early humans and our primate ancestors and relatives, most notably chimpanzees. How much of the territoriality expressed by early foragers, for instance, is traceable to a primate inheritance, and how much to contingent factors such as resource distribution or increasing population density? Or to rephrase the question, we might ask "how and when a territorial definition of society changed to a social definition of territory" (Sampson 1988:16).

Core/periphery organization can be discerned in even the simplest of groups, but the nature of both core and periphery, as well as the relationship between them, vary considerably not only synchronically, but also with the evolution of sociocultural complexity. Since kin-based systems of dominance and/or exploitation are inherently unstable, core/periphery systems under these circumstances are difficult to establish and maintain and therefore tend to be fairly minimal and short-lived; this generally restricts semi-sedentary foragers to episodic raiding and more or less ephemeral control over desirable areas beyond a core area. There seems to be a correlation between the development of hierarchies based upon increased stratification and the organization and centralization of power and the ability of states and empires to exercise control through the exaction of taxes and tribute from peripheral societies. Thus early or "pristine" states should, according to this hypothesis, be more successful at acquiring resources from peripheries than kin-based systems, but not as much as later centralized empires (Parker Pearson 1989:27–28).

Early boundaries tended to be diffuse and permeable. For much of human prehistory foraging groups were widely separated, rarely came into contact with other groups, and tended to retreat when they did so rather than behave territorially. Wide buffer zones or no-man's-land separated groups and the outer limits were rarely crossed (Sampson 1988:15). The nature and function of boundaries clearly changed with two epochal developments in human organization: the domestication of plants and animals and the rise of the state (cf. Kratochwil 1986:87). As groups became increasingly sedentary, they also became more territorial as the meaning and value of land and land ownership changed. Consequently buffer zones decreased in width and boundaries were more definitively marked by the digging of ditches and the erection of cairns or boundary markers; burials were also used to mark the edge of defensible settlement (Fischer 1949:217; Dodgshon 1987:68; cf. Renfrew 1976).

Having explored some of the general evolutionary principles of territoriality and spatial organization, let us now look more specifically at different phases of human sociocultural development. For this purpose I utilize Service's typological sequence of political organization— i.e., band, tribe, chiefdom and state (1962)—as a rough index of increasing social, political and economic complexity.

Initially territoriality was limited to fairly small core areas inhabited by small nomadic groups; such core areas crucially included a water source and possibly one or more key food resources. Boundaries were either nonexistent or extremely diffuse, representing the outermost limits of foraging, while hunters routinely ranged beyond such limits, but laid no claim to the territories they hunted in. Core and periphery existed, but both were quite rudimentary and ill-defined, particularly the periphery. Essentially everything beyond the limits of daily foraging activity was the periphery, either uninhabited by other humans or occupied by the Other (cf. Bonzani 1992:211). As the number and size of hunting and gathering groups increased, more contact occurred among them, particularly in resource-rich environments— such as during the European Mesolithic—leading to increased territorial behavior, including exclusive rights to land and boundary defense (Dodgshon 1987:37–38).

Not surprisingly, the world view of earlier and simpler societies was more circumscribed, and correspondingly the conception of space was more limited. As Eliade notes:

> In archaic and traditional societies, the surrounding world is conceived as a microcosm. At the limits of this closed world begins the domain of the unknown, of the formless. On this side there is ordered—because inhabited and organized—space; on the other, outside this familiar

space, there is the unknown and dangerous region of the demons, the ghosts, the dead and of foreigners—in a word, chaos or death or night. This image of an inhabited microcosm, surrounded by desert regions regarded as a chaos or a kingdom of the dead, has survived even in highly evolved civilisations such as those of China, Mesopotamia and Egypt. Indeed, a good many texts liken the enemies who are attacking national territory to ghosts, demons or the powers of chaos [1952:37–38; cf. Helms 1988:30; Patterson 1977:43].

The first major shift in territoriality and spatial organization accompanied the domestication of plants and animals. For those groups which emphasized the domestication of animals and developed the specialized economic orientation of nomadic pastoralism, this required fewer modifications of spatial concepts other than increased attention to protection of flocks and assurance of sufficient grazing. In the nomadic domain the use of land depends on the type of grazing, quality and quantity of water supply and the type of animal exploited; land use is therefore essentially complementary and territory non-exclusive. The tribal area is a functional rather than a formal political region and the boundary is reflected in terms of social groups with exclusive access to an economic zone rather than a sovereign ownership of territory (Wilkinson 1983:308).

However, for those societies which gradually became more and more sedentary, their relationship with the land altered more radically. As population density increases—one major consequence of the shift from foraging to agriculture, especially in areas of rich, well-watered arable land—territories tend to become smaller and more compact due to the increased availability and reliability of resources, boundaries become more distinct and buffer zones are created (Sampson 1988:25; Bonzani 1992:211). "With the emergence of farming, we can say that territoriality acquired a sharper edge to it as territories slowly became segments of space over which groups established exclusive rights of access and use and in which they had invested labour.... Signs of this heightened sense of territoriality are provided by the appearance of man-made boundaries and boundary-markers of a more symbolic sort" (Dodgshon 1987:67).

The shift from foraging to agriculture also led to the first real disparity in subsistence strategy and consequently in land use. For the first time groups could be exploiting the same land, but were not necessarily competing for the same resources. However, the differing land use would have, and did, lead to conflict (Gregg 1988). Moreover, the growth in population created by sedentary agriculturalists led to land hunger and expansion of farmers and herders at the expense of hunters and gatherers, setting in motion the moving agricultural frontier, which usually proceeded to occupy all available arable land until a more stable border between agriculturalists and foragers was established (Alexander 1977:28; cf. Bogucki 1987). Two of the more prominent examples of this kind of moving frontier were the northwestern movement of Neolithic farmers in Europe beginning around the seventh millennium BC and the much later westward advancement of the North American frontier, but this process occurred in a similar fashion wherever the domestication of plants and animals occurred.

More complex social and political relationships emerged with sedentism, leading to the formation of tribal societies, societies still based on kinship, but also with a corporate sense of territoriality. "The tribe is always a territorial unit" (Linton 1936:232). Separating tribal territories—the boundaries of which still tended to be relatively diffuse and ill-defined compared to later state boundaries—were wide swaths of no man's land or buffer zones which were normally unoccupied and unclaimed (Hickerson 1965:43; cf. Thornton 1982).

Because of their emphasis on kin-based social cohesion rather than political control or organization, tribes are inherently unstable and their territories are equivalently unstable as well; tribes routinely fragment, disperse and reform, more often as the result of internal conflict than external pressure. Chiefdoms, however, have the potential for greater stability resulting from the authority of the chief and a supportive kin-based hierarchy. Chiefdoms therefore possessed the capability of limited expansion, with greater population and territorial extent than tribes, although their geographical limits still tended to represent social limits as well (Dodgshon 1987:135). On the other hand, as Stein (1998:6) suggests, such polities are perhaps best viewed as "fuzzy networks with poorly defined and contingent boundaries formed through differential and constantly shifting patterns of cooperation and competition among emergent elites and other groups." Chiefdoms also relied upon unoccupied buffer zones to limit social interaction and function as defensive barriers (Bonzani 1992:213).

The second major development which resulted in a considerable modification of spatial concepts was the rise of the state, which ulti-mately led to the formation of empires and world systems. With state societies came a shift away from a reliance on kinship as a means of social and political integration toward the creation of more centralized forms of social and political control and organization and thus a tran-sition from a social definition of territory to a territorially-defined soci-ety (Dodgshon 1987:130). "For this reason, we can expect the character of core-periphery systems to have evolved in step with the changing character of societal order, the one being the organisational imprint of the other. Thus, as simple chiefdoms evolved into systems of chiefdoms and the chiefdoms into states, so also, can we expect core-periphery structures to have evolved into more complex and qualitatively differ-ent forms" (Dodgshon 1987:242).

Or as Soja puts it, "the emergence of the state marked the first time that the territorial organization of society came to be defined extensively in terms of formally delimited regions" (1971:34). Whereas boundaries of pre-state polities tended to be diffuse, shifting and ill-defined, state or geopolitical boundaries gradually coalesced from zones to precisely defined and defended lines. Thus, "borders in the context of state societies are a radically different kind of thing than they are in the context of band, tribal, and chiefdom societies. The extent of boundary marking reflects the need to control flows between two political entities" (Price 1973:162).

The earliest states therefore represent a prototype of center/ periphery organization, originating for the most part in rich alluvial river valleys and expanding to encompass territory of a similar nature until the limits of effective cultivation and/or political control were reached. The outer boundary of control eventually became a recog-nized and tangible separation between the border—the furthest extent of state occupation and authority—and the frontier, more marginal land occupied by other peoples, most of whom were at least initially less powerful and less highly organized. In the normal evolution of states, eventually the core begins to decline and, according to the Law of Evolutionary Potential, peripheral societies often emerge to super-sede them (Service 1960; Giddens et al. 1973; Paynter 1981:119).

As other states came into existence, not only did they establish borders and boundaries with other states, but peer polity interaction— primarily in terms of trade or conflict—also led to the formation of the first world systems. "World system," however, had a somewhat different context in the Bronze Age than in the modern world, since the known inhabited world was not global, but rather more restricted in scope. A second consequence of state expansion was the formation of empires, which extended the scope and scale of territorial expansion. Both world systems and empires thus comprise the most elaborate and fully-developed center/periphery systems.

4

Border and Frontier Processes

Political Processes

Many of the political processes in peripheral zones, like those in core zones, are concerned with aspects of power and control. Most, indeed, as will be seen, involve relationships between core and periphery and variables including the complexity of contact and interaction, the extent of economic activity, and the ability of a group or entire society to monopolize the acquisition, production, and/or distribution of crucial resources (Schortman and Urban 1992:245). I will begin with aspects of political evolution since they often originate in the center and extend into the periphery, and then I will discuss other variables which create or affect political processes.

Centralization is one such process. Not only does centralization involve the gathering and focusing of power and authority in a central individual or institution, but it also entails the progressive spatial extension of control in the core area and into the periphery. And according to the centripetal model of spatial organization, centralization tends to increase as one approaches the core and decrease as one moves outward into the periphery (Haselgrove 1984:16), partly at least as the effect of distance decay, e.g., increasing cost and ease of communication and transport.

Secondary state formation is another process, whereby contact with and influence from a more developed and politically complex core state leads to political development in the periphery (Haselgrove 1984; Bloemers 1988:13, 1989:177). Thus, the appearance of a ranked or stratified polity within an interaction network tends to be followed by shifts toward increased complexity among its contact partners. In part this follows from the demands the complex polity puts on its neighbors to organize for the production and/or transport of needed social valuables. Sociopolitical hierarchies also develop as "peripheral" scions take advantage of opportunities to acquire and monopolize new sources of wealth provided by their complex partners [Schortman and Urban 1992:244].

Local elites play a key role in this process by establishing social and economic contacts and relationships with core elites, often leading subsequently to political alliances and connections. By virtue of the prestige, wealth and authority gained through such relationships, these local elites are often able to increase their political power and control, enabling centralization to occur in the periphery (Haselgrove 1984), ultimately resulting in the transformation of tribes into chiefdoms and chiefdoms into small states. As core states decline and collapse, these emergent peripheral states often then take advantage of such developments to increase their own size, control and power. Any effort to assert, expand or maintain political power and control almost inevitably leads to conflict, another process endemic to and closely associated with borders and frontiers.

Although focusing predominantly on economic processes, the world systems core/periphery model also deals extensively with political relationships between center and periphery. In this model, the center is comprised of one or more strong centralized state authorities. Since land tenure was the overriding political mechanism by which people competed for power, the core zone tended to develop in areas with rich soil, central location, and a large labor force (Cohen and Maier 1983:292). Since spatial organization mirrors sociopolitical organization, this form of political organization can be contrasted with traditional non-centralized societies with a fluid arrangement of functional regions shaped by the character and structure of the kinship system, by local ecological factors, and by the pattern of inter-group relations. Thus, "one of the most important developments in human social and political organization comes about when localized kinship or residence groups become territorial units within a political system" (Soja 1971:13).

Given the general principle that the strength of political control and authority diminishes with distance, the classical form of the core/periphery model is one of concentric circles, whereby, in its fullest development—i.e., that of an empire or hegemonic state:

> The core, usually the area of earliest political consolidation, continued to be ruled directly by the central authority. Then came an inner area of closely assimilated and politically integrated dependencies. Beyond it was the circle of relatively secure vassal polities and ... "subordinate allies" who enjoyed a certain degree of autonomy. This circle merged with the next circle of tribute-paying polities straining at the center's political leash. Beyond, the center's control became increasingly symbolic, confining itself to fewer and fewer functions. Increasingly, the etiquette of domination prevailed over its substance. And beyond a certain point, control became erratic, ineffective and, finally impossible—in the way of classical "marches." The center could only practice political intimidation and extract sporadic tribute through institutionalized raiding or undisguised pillage. Finally, came the potential frontier—areas beyond the effective reach of the metropolitan power, which nevertheless sometimes conceitedly claimed to control it [Kopytoff 1987:29].

Where large states, empires or world systems existed, peripheries tended to be more diverse than those of smaller and less complex polities, with different levels and manifestations of political organization ranging from acephalous tribes to highly centralized states. Different peripheries therefore might necessitate different methods of political control or interaction, such as direct vs. indirect rule, conquest vs. alliance, etc. Political structures and processes in borders and frontiers tend to differ as well, given varying degrees of integration into the core political system. Different areas or zones within the periphery of the same core state or states might as a result involve different political and associated economic processes. Examples of this phenomenon abound in the archaeological and historical records, but some of the clearest evidence for the diversity of political responses can be seen in the Roman empire, which encountered German tribes, Celtic chiefdoms, Hellenistic states and the Carthaginian empire, among others, during the course of its expansion (Haselgrove 1984; Hedeager 1987).

Though political processes rarely occur in isolation, their association in a periphery with other kinds of processes is not always patterned or predictable. Thus a particular political organization does not necessarily imply an equivalent economic, social or cultural structure. Economic influence, for example, does not always involve political control, nor does political dominance necessarily involve acculturation or assimilation, although sometimes these processes accompany or follow from political control.

The limits of political control or authority are indicated by or manifested in political boundaries. The nature and enforcement of such boundaries varies considerably according to contingencies such as distance, geography and the sociopolitical complexity of the societies in contact. Political boundaries, however, are primarily an artifact of the state, and those of less complexly organized polities therefore tend to be less consistently recognized or implemented. Initially such boundaries have no more strength or permanence than internal divisions, but as the size and power of the state increases, so does the distinction between internal and external boundaries (e.g., Sahlins 1989). Political boundaries indicate or are meant to indicate political unity within while denoting separation from adjoining polities (Kristof 1959:281; Cherry 1987).

Although a primary function of political boundaries is to restrict and control movement, they can nonetheless be quite permeable; some permeability may be determined by the government, while other variables such as location, geography and the nature of the boundary, the peoples separated by the boundary, and the amount of effort and resources expended also influence the nature and amount of movement and communication. Even boundaries designed and built to represent considerable barriers such as Hadrian's Wall, the Great Wall of China and the Berlin Wall were not totally impermeable, and in the first two instances, were not meant to be.

Just as political processes do not necessarily or always accompany other kinds of processes, political boundaries often do not coincide with ethnic or cultural boundaries. In fact, modern political boundaries notoriously cut through tribal, cultural, and ethnic boundaries, separating members from each other (Trigger 1974:98–99; Elton 1996:27; Liverani 1987:66). For this and related reasons, political boundaries are one of the primary sources of conflict between polities or groups (Kapil 1966:256–258; Martinez 1988:4). Unlike other kinds of boundaries, which tend to be diffuse and at times difficult to discern, modern political boundaries are usually discrete, sharply and abruptly demarcating the end of effective jurisdiction.

Thus, a boundary by its very nature is alien to the life of the zone it bisects. The usual effect of locating a boundary on an ongoing interaction system is to create relative discontinuities where none had existed. Conflict potential is, therefore, related to the degree of disruptive impact a boundary has on its environment (Kapil 1966:657).

On the other hand, though less commonly, ethnic, cultural, national and political identities could, as Sahlins notes, under the right conditions, reinforce each other:

> The formation of the national territorial boundary line and the expression of national identities ... were two-way processes. The states did not simply impose the boundary or the nation on local society. By defining their own social and territorial boundaries, village communities, peasants and notables made use of the national state and its boundaries. By repeatedly using their nations, by bringing the nation into the village, members of local society ended up as national citizens [1989:276].

Beyond the boundary of the border, the limit of effective political control or jurisdiction, lies the frontier (Wyman and Kroeber 1965:xiii). The frontier is the land of the Other, a different polity or polities at a minimum, and possibly a different political system or structure as well. According to Kristof (1959), the frontier is characterized by rudimentary sociopolitical relations marked by rebelliousness, lawlessness and/or the absence of laws. As open territory, the frontier can be penetrated and occupied—either transiently or permanently—by individuals or groups, remaining a frontier until effective or formal military or political control is established, at which point the area ceases to be a frontier and becomes a border.

Borders and frontiers both can function as buffer zones, i.e., intermediate regions which are interposed between the core zone and other areas considered valuable and central and any form of external threat. Buffer zones in the frontier can serve as a no man's land in which no polity exercises control and which is in theory accessible to more than one group, though not necessarily at the same time (Hickerson 1965; Kopytoff 1987:29). Hostile encounters might occur between individuals or groups of varying size without necessarily invoking the power of the state or a formal response, or they might alternatively represent the sporadic opening phases of a wider and more serious conflict. The ideal configuration of a buffer zone is for a military force to be powerful enough to deter an attack through their territory, but not strong or

4. Border and Frontier Processes

hostile enough to represent a threat of their own to the center. Empires therefore often created buffer zones by establishing allies or tributary states on their borders (Lee 1970; Hedeager 1979:207, 1987:126–129). Whether groups on the border or in the frontier were treated as barriers or threats as opposed to friends and allies depended on variables such as geography, distance and the nature of the groups (Hall 2000:251).

Buffer zones can also be seen as a kind of border between different ecological niches, particularly land suitable for agriculture on the one hand and pastoralism or foraging on the other (Leach 1960). The boundaries of such border zones may fluctuate according both to climatic and political conditions. When the environment is favorable for sedentary habitation and when political control is strong, centralized, and expansive, more of the buffer zone is settled; when political control is weaker and/or the land is less suitable for farming, the territory is dominated by nomadic peoples (Finklestein 1995:67).

Borders tend to be less centralized than the core, but more so than the frontier. Thus border dwellers are pulled more weakly to the center and more strongly to the bordering population on the other side of the boundary separating them. As the core polity becomes more complex and centralized, the boundaries on either side of the border also change, becoming more precisely defined and more strongly enforced. On the United States-Mexico border, for example,

> although the border separated Mexican Americans politically from Mexico, physical proximity kept them tied to their roots culturally and socially. Those continuing links to the motherland shaped to a significant degree their marginality within American society. Their compatriots across the Rio Grande or on Mexican soil found themselves insulated from American political domination but not from economic and cultural influences; that reality, coupled with sheer geographic remoteness from the core of the nation, assured that the *nortenos* and *fronterizos* (borderlanders) would develop social patterns distinct from the rest of Mexico. Thus the presence of the border played a fundamental role in converting border Chicanos and Mexicans into entities that stood apart from the mainstream societies of each nation [Martinez 1988:5; cf. Bustamonte 1992].

The creation of buffer zones represents one form of political expansion, while incorporation involves another political and/or military solution to internal political problems and/or external threats or opportunities. While buffer zones essentially leave indigenous societies and institutions in place, incorporation necessitates structural changes, alterations in political identity, loss of autonomy and subordination to a higher and more powerful authority (Hall 2000:251). On their northern periphery, for example, the Romans incorporated those Celtic societies whose political structure and organization was sufficiently developed and centralized to resemble their own, created buffer zones in more distant regions where Celtic chiefdoms existed, and excluded the even more distant, more hostile and unassimilable Germanic tribes (Headeger 1979, 1987). Political expansion takes place in the frontier and the process of incorporation ultimately results in the end of the frontier, which becomes a border (cf. Thompson and Lamar 1981).

The highest level of political evolution is the empire and/or world system, a highly centralized polity with the greatest population, territorial extent and levels of integration, i.e., core, border and frontier or core, semi-periphery, and periphery (cf. Cherry 1987; Sinopoli 1994). Empires evolve from states and derive their complexity from expansion—in this context imperialism—and the incorporation of diverse peoples and territories.

The political structure of empires therefore differs from that of other complex states as much in its ability to incorporate local power structures as in its central hierarchy. The interest here is not in the diversity of local administrative forms but in the strategies used to bind these to the political structure of the empire. These strategies linking centralized and local power structures contain the mechanisms of expansion of empires (Trinkaus 1984:35).

Indirect rule is another method of establishing control in peripheries whereby local rulers or leaders are left in place with considerable authority but acknowledge the overlordship of an imperial state, paying tribute for the privilege of remaining in power and/or cementing their alliance or relationship through marriage (Cherry 1987). This method was extensively employed by the Persian and Roman empires in the ancient world and the British empire in modern times.

Many if not most political processes involve the activities of an elite class or those who aspire to that status. In the core zone most political structures and processes are initiated by and are for the benefit of the ruling elite, including most of the processes described above

4. Border and Frontier Processes

such as expansion, centralization and incorporation. Local elites or would-be elites in peripheries look to the center not only for connections to enhance their status, wealth and/or power but also as models for their own political control (Wells 1980, 1987, 1998; Gerstle 1984; Demarest 1988; Woolf 1990, 1998; Kristiansen and Larsson 2005), thus promoting the kind of secondary state development discussed above.

It is often quite difficult, as noted above, to disentangle such political processes from economic and social ones, since aspects of wealth, prestige and power intertwine as well. One example is what Dietler terms "commensal politics," "the manipulation of commensal hospitality as a means of defining relations of relative power and status in social contexts" (1998:305). Ceremonial and ritualized feasting, and especially drinking, serves to enhance and maintain political authority through redistributive hospitality and tribute (Dietler 1997, 2005).

One of the most common forms of political action in peripheries is conflict (Peattie 1944; Alvarez 1995; cf. Rice 1998). Contact and interaction with the Other leads, as noted elsewhere, to a range of possible encounters, and conflict under such conditions is almost inevitable (Cusick 1998). As individuals or groups enter new territory already occupied by different individuals or groups, conflicts arise over the occupation of land and the exploitation of resources such as water, timber or minerals. As immigration increases, so does the level of stress and conflict (Thompson and Lamar 1981):

> In frontier zones, contention occurs at two interrelated levels. First, frontiersmen from both the societies of the invader and the invaded continue their *intra*mural contention. Along frontiers, new opportunities for spoils often intensify these internal struggles for power and, in the case of state societies, the weak moderating influence of distant central governments also permits intramural contention to escalate unchecked. Second, *inter*mural contention, unique to societies that face one another along frontiers, gives rise to cultural conflict [Weber 1992:12–13].

Conflict may take place between groups practicing the same form of economic exploitation—i.e., foraging, pastoralism or agriculture—involving competition for the same land or resources, or conflict may ensue between different modes of exploitation, most notably foraging and agriculture (Dodgshon 1987). The introduction or spread of agriculture in a region almost always results in conflict, particularly at the

interface between two economic systems, such as the margins of extensive cultivation where the expansion of agriculture tends to be at the
expense of the best potential grazing (Wilkinson 1983; Grahame 1998).
Efforts at political or economic incorporation also routinely lead
to conflict as indigenous peoples react to and resist change (Ezell 1961;
Hall 2000:241). Conflict may result from competition for material
goods introduced by early representatives of more developed societies
or by the imposition of different belief systems.

> Gradually ... members of the indigenous society may become aware that
> the intrusion constitutes danger to their autonomy and identity. This
> process of erosion is often intensified by an increase in the number of
> intruders and by the arrival of new categories of intruders, especially of
> settlers—as when farmers followed missionaries and peripatetic traders
> into the interior of North America and southern Africa with the mani-
> fest intention of becoming permanent inhabitants of the region. In such
> cases there then ensues a more or less open conflict for use of the natu-
> ral resources of the region—land and water supplies—and eventually for
> physical control over the entire territory and all its inhabitants
> [Thompson and Lamar 1981:9–10].

The creation, imposition, shifting and/or maintenance of boundaries also represents fertile ground for conflict (Osborne 1987). Political
boundaries, as noted above, often, if not usually, cut across social, cultural and ethnic boundaries, thus dividing groups and establishing dis-
junctions between them (Kapil 1966:656–657; cf. Pellow 1996). The
coincidence of political boundaries with natural ones also influences
the potential for conflict; boundaries which follow mountain peaks,
for example, induce less opportunity for conflict due to their remoteness and low population density compared to boundaries tracking river
banks (Kratochwil 1986). Border and boundary disputes not only usually involve peoples of different race, culture or ethnicity, but also
invoke tribal or state authorities in addition to local ones (Sahlins
1989:233).

Class conflict between elite and non-elite elements of society tends
to be greater in peripheries because local elites in peripheries largely
monopolize and benefit from contact and interaction with the center
at the expense of non-elites, while non-elites in the core zone receive
at least some of the benefits of state or imperial exploitation of the
periphery (Bloemers 1988).

Eventually much of the conflict generated in peripheries results in violent aggression, beginning with fights between individuals and small groups, skirmishes and raids, and sometimes rising to the level of warfare. The expansion of states and empires into frontiers or the borderlands of other states or empires clearly represents the occasion for frequent warfare, in addition to conflicts between state and non-state societies in the "tribal zone" interface (Ferguson and Whitehead 1992; Hall 2000:241). However, as the frontier closes because the limit of expansion has been reached, state or imperial aggression is usually replaced with a more defensive posture focusing on protecting the borders rather than extending them, as occurred with the Roman and Chinese empires (e.g., Barfield 1989; Williams 1998).

Since warfare was one of the primary means of acquiring slaves, and since border and frontier conflicts involved the Other—i.e., inhabitants of the periphery—the acquisition of slaves was often the byproduct of conflicts carried out for other reasons and sometimes the primary cause of raids for that purpose alone (e.g., Nash 1985).

Economic Processes

Since world systems theory deals preeminently with economic structures and relationships, I will begin my discussion of economic processes in peripheries with a more detailed description and analysis of this influential model. In the modern world system the core is comprised of one or more strong state societies with highly-developed technology and sophisticated economic institutions, while the periphery is underdeveloped, with weak political structure, minimal technological development and decentralized economic structures. Thus the relationship between core and periphery is profoundly asymmetrical, whereby the center dominates and controls the periphery (Wallerstein 1974).

Dominance of center over periphery usually begins by monopolizing some crucial aspect of interregional exchange relations, such as finished goods, transportation or military power leading to the accumulation of capital which can fund core expansion. Core control is further strengthened when peripheries supply different elements of products made in centralized workshops, thus enabling core elites to dictate terms of exchange and reducing economic decision-makers to a small number of state leaders (Schortman and Urban 1994:404). Between center and periphery lies the semi-periphery, which links and integrates core and periphery while also functioning as a buffer between them (Champion 1989:6). In theory, then, centers and peripheries exist along a continuum of differential access to raw materials, status-related goods, and transport costs. The core is wealthy and relatively densely populated, characterized by good access to trade routes and various resources, while the periphery is more sparsely populated, undeveloped, and oriented toward monoculture and transportation networks linking it to the core area (Lerner 1987:98, 114).

> Neither core or periphery is considered an autonomous, isolated entity; the linkage between them is part of a feedback relationship in which the core dominates the periphery, forming a pattern of dynamic interaction; in general the periphery is viewed as an underdeveloped area to be systematically exploited by the core; to this end the core controls not only all external trade of the periphery but also the division of labor and access to resources; thus viewed, peripheries exist in a dependent relationship with the core due to the unequal distribution of socially necessary resources and the domination of exchange relations and labor [Lerner 1987:98].

More specifically, the subsistence economy of the center is dominated by intensive grain cropping in rich soil, often employing irrigation, while the agriculture of the periphery tends to involve rainfall-dependent extensive farming and pastoralism in more marginal lands. Frontiers are, on the other hand, characterized by abundant non-agricultural resources such as timber and minerals which are exploited as raw materials by the core (Dodgshon 1987:280). While the nature and structure of cores are generally similar, there is considerably greater variation in the nature of peripheries, as well as in the degree of control and/or integration between center and periphery; for example, the extent of incorporation ranges from complete economic domination to informal interaction with isolated and independent areas, with the majority falling somewhere in between (Eccles 1983:127; Lerner 1987:98; Fulford 1989:90; Ucko 1989:xv; Santley and Alexander 1992:31; Schon and Galaty 2006:252). Variables of incorporation would include aspects such as: the amount of goods exchanged; the types of goods; the amount of labor involved in their production; whether they are raw products, manufactured goods, or prestige goods; degree of centralization of the exchange process; and relative importance of the transfer to each economy (Hall 2000:242).

Given that borders, and particularly frontiers, tend to be fluid rather than stable, it follows that there should be evolutionary processes whereby the relationship between center and periphery changes, often in predictable ways. Demand from the core for specific foods, materials or products leads over time to peripheries moving away from a diversified generalized subsistence economy toward functional specialization in particular crops, natural resources or items (DeAtley 1984:9; Ucko 1989:xv; Stein 1998:231). This results in increasing dependence of the periphery on the center for food, tools and other finished products (Groenman-van Wateringe 1983:148). One well-documented example of this process is the North American fur trade. In the 17th and 18th centuries AD, furs were not an essential import to the European nation states, but there was a strong and growing demand for them that encouraged Native American tribes to focus more and more of their attention on obtaining furs for trade with the European market, ultimately leading to

> major social and economic changes among indigenous groups, including dependency on European goods, which led to expansion of hunting which increased warfare and depleted the environment; the nature of warfare changed, including greater dependence on guns; intensified harvesting of furs led to dispersion of families during winter in pursuit of animals, which left women at home in charge of camps while men were absent for long periods; increased travel and contact helped spread diseases, often long before contact with Europeans [Hall 2000:243; cf. Thomas 1985].

On the other hand, under different circumstances,

> ... as the core comes to depend on products from the periphery their domination of the relationship decreases, with the effect that core and periphery move toward a relationship of mutual interdependence which evolves through a feedback cycle in which complexity in the periphery is accelerated through the acquisition of finished goods from the core combined with the creation of additional markets for export production; thus augmenting the level of interregional trade between the two areas may lead to local economic growth and development in the periphery [Lerner 1987:98; cf. Cherry 1987:20; Millett 1990:39–40; Santley and Alexander 1992:32; Nelson 1993:177; Stein 1998:229–230].

Another possible outcome results from the development of improved markets, leading in turn to increased food production and larger population, causing increased demand for foodstuffs, and thus placing greater pressure on farmers for agricultural production using traditional agricultural methods (Groenman-van Waateringe 1983:149; cf. Smith 1998:261). Some of the demand for food arises from growth of craft production and the administrators required to supervise it, leading in the long term to "the creation of a centralized political economy integrating local production with intra- and intersocietal systems of exchange" (Schortman and Urban 1994:403).

The development of long-distance trade, which stimulated interregional exchange, has also been implicated as an agent of cultural evolution, particularly in respect to the appearance of trade specialists and market communities (Sharer 1977:66; Hirth 1978:36; Tartaron 2001:28). A related development is the creation of a semi-periphery in border zones which functions as an intermediary between center and periphery in such trade, leading to increased population and prosperity, as well as expansion into the frontier (Foster 1986:63; Rowlands and Frankenstein 1998:342). Thus, there is a variety of potential developmental trajectories ranging from more or less complete economic domination and exploitation of the periphery by the core to eventual growth, development and autonomy by a periphery whereby it becomes the core of a new world system.

As discussed earlier, world systems theory has been criticized on various grounds (e.g., Strassaldo 1980:42–43; Ragin and Chirot 1984:303), but here I will focus upon economic aspects of precapitalist societies. Much of the discussion forms part of the larger formalist/substantist debate initiated by Polanyi (e.g., 1944) which has roiled the fields of economics and anthropology for several generations and concerns *inter alia* the role and function of long-distance trade, particularly in respect to social relationships (Smith 1998:261).

A more significant critique of world systems theory as articulated by Wallerstein (1974) and others concerns the extent to which peripheries were dependent upon and controlled by core states in the ancient world. Since transportation and productive technologies were less highly developed than today, it was more difficult for the center to control areas at any distance; this lack of control also enabled peripheral societies to develop complex institutions more easily than in the mod-

4. Border and Frontier Processes

ern world. According to Kohl (1987:20–21), *interdependency* better describes the relationship of Bronze Age polities than dependency; although less developed peripheral societies were more strongly affected by participation in exchange networks than ancient civilizations, they nevertheless had a range of options from withdrawal to substitution of trade partners not generally available in the modern world (cf. Millett 1970:7; Smith 1998:261).

One well-studied ancient economic world system is the Greco-Roman world and its interaction with various barbarian societies, which according to Cunliffe (1988:200) comprised (1) ports-of-trade or gateway communities at their interface; (2) an intermediate zone with a market economy directly linked to them; (3) an elite redistribution zone; and (4) a procurement zone from which raw materials and labor were obtained (cf. Millett 1970:7; Woolf 1990). The Roman system, a complex of exchange networks based primarily on gift exchange, remained relatively small and stable during the early Republic, but then underwent a radical reorganization and expansion with Rome's transition from a city state to an empire (Cunliffe 1988:7).

By the 2nd century AD the world system encompassed by the Roman empire involved an inner core of Italy which consumed raw materials and manpower well in excess of its productive capacity in order to maintain an elaborate state apparatus and high urban population and supported by taxation and tribute; an inner periphery of rich provinces (Spain, Gaul, Africa and Asia) producing far in excess of local needs, part of which went to the center and part to defense of the borders; and the barbarian periphery from which raw materials and manpower were obtained. The system, however, was in a state of unstable equilibrium leading to potential collapse due to factors including fluctuation in the supply of luxury goods and conflicts between the elite redistribution zone and the procurement zone (Cunliffe 1988:200; cf. Lattimore 1979:38–39).

Having sketched the "big picture" world economic system, I now turn my attention to specific aspects of that system, first in terms of different aspects of center and periphery and then in various economic processes. Since core economic processes are relatively well known compared to peripheral ones, I will focus here primarily on elements of the periphery—borders, frontiers and colonies—and refer to the center only to the extent that it concerns the periphery as well.

Boundaries, Borders and Frontiers in Archaeology

Borders, as noted earlier, functioned *inter alia* as economic transition or intermediate zones between the more developed center and less-developed peripheries (e.g., Cifani et al. 2012:169). The extent of dependence on the core varied according local circumstances, but for the most part border zones were relatively self-contained and self-sufficient (Fulford 1989:90). Enterprising local elites in these areas created roles for themselves as middlemen, brokering the exchange of finished products from the core with raw materials and luxury goods from the periphery while enriching themselves and enhancing their status and political control in the process (Paynter 1981). Border markets between a settled core society and frontier pastoralists were useful and profitable for parties on both sides, but were often controlled or adjusted to prevent too much trade and economic integration on one hand and too limited trade on the other, which might provoke excessive raiding, as on China's northern border (Lattimore 1962:481; Barfield 1989:9, 2001:19). Trade in Roman border zones most often involved items of everyday use and Roman coinage, while those destined for the frontier beyond tended to be—both because of increased transportation costs and demand by barbarian elites—luxury goods (mostly vessels connected with eating and drinking, some of precious metal, notably silver coins and glassware) obtained through exchange, thus involving different systems of value and exchange mechanisms (Hedeager 1979:216; Whittaker 1983:116, 1994:125; Fulford 1985:100, 1989:85; Wells 1992:185; cf. Woolf 1998:180).

At borders between two or more centers local elites were also often able to manipulate the flow of goods and services to take advantage of supply and demand from each center, as well as supplying them from the border region. In addition, "extra-urban sanctuaries in Etruria and *Magna Graecia* were, quite commonly, built as landmarks of frontiers and many frontier sanctuaries had also a secondary value as *emporia*, places where trade and exchanges between people of different communities were admitted under the protection of the local gods" (Cifani et al. 2012:169). Modern state boundaries tend, in most cases, to be strictly maintained and enforced, a practice which may emphasize disparities in economic conditions and policies, and these differences may be exploited in various ways. Tariffs, taxes, restrictions and embargoes on imports and exports create imbalances in the quantity and value of goods, giving rise to smuggling, i.e., the illegal or impermissible

4. Border and Frontier Processes

movement of people and things. The smuggling of drugs in particular has become widespread and highly profitable in the modern world, but almost anything identified as contraband may receive similar treatment.

The creation of an economic administrative structure in Roman border provinces—which was usually more an expansion of the existing system rather than the opening of a new one—generally had several consequences, including the modification of previous regional exchange patterns, the opening of new markets for products from other parts of the empire, and the economic impact of the presence of the army as consumer. These developments in turn led to a considerable increase in the number of private merchants. When the boundaries of the empire stabilized, a more settled exchange pattern developed; although trans-border activity continued, new and more distant markets in the frontier appeared as well (Elton 1996:77).

From an economic perspective frontiers represent outlying regions potentially rich in resources (Strassoldo 1977:87) which can be exploited through mining or other means of extraction or harvesting (Dyson 1985:274–275). Obviously one valuable resource is land itself, and the attraction of "free" land has always been a significant component of movement into such open areas (Smith 1950:4–5). People, too, comprise a resource in various ways, not the least as a source of labor, unfree or otherwise. In addition to crops unavailable in the core zone, other desirable resources include minerals and timber. The consequences of such exploitation could be considerable. In Gaul, for instance, raiding and looting caused by increasing Roman demands for slaves and raw materials disrupted the stability of Celtic tribes, although others in more direct contact with Rome often benefited economically (Cunliffe 1988:92).

Again, the Roman economic world system offers illustration of the roles, functions and distinctions of core, border and frontier, with my emphasis here on frontiers. As we have seen, the core was the center of production and consumption and its border regions functioned as markets and middlemen for both raw materials and finished products. Beyond the boundaries of the empire lay the barbarian world which supplied raw materials and slaves and whose tribal elites represented a market for luxury goods (Whittaker 1983:114–116); aside from this long-distance trade, however, economic interaction between border

63

and frontier was quite limited (Fulford 1989:91–92). In other words, indigenous decision-makers in the frontier zone chose those aspects of Roman material culture that appealed to them from a limited selection of options and were not economically dependent upon Rome otherwise (Woolf 1998:180). The contrast in this respect between borders and frontiers is articulated by Fulford (1985:100):

> In the first century AD the source of the prestigious goods was mainly Italy and southern Gaul but, as provincial workshops developed, more and more objects originated from these. The prestigious items are found in graves or in hoards—often deposited in bogs—or as unassociated finds. In stark contrast the objects of the "buffer trade" are usually found in settlements and their associated cemeteries. Altogether the range of finds from the "buffer zone" is comparable to that from rural settlements *within* the Limes, although quantities may vary considerably.

As Whittaker notes, the boundary between border and frontier—i.e., the limit of effective Roman control—was found at "a marginal zone of switchover from intensive to extensive food production" (1989:66; cf. Lattimore 1962). Initially, different frontier zones in the Roman periphery had different kinds of economic organization, but by the 2nd and mid–3rd centuries AD, as they were more fully integrated into the Roman economic system, many of these differences were minimized (Fulford 1989:84–85). During the early phases of the empire most Romans in the frontier not part of the military were traders of some sort whose primary market was the army, but eventually they were assimilated into the indigenous population (Elton 1996:7–8).

Colonies, as noted earlier, represent a particular kind of frontier, and although their establishment was due to a variety of factors including population pressure and the need to secure strategic locales, the primary motivation for the founding of most colonies was economic. In some cases their function was restricted to the extraction of a specific resource such as cattle, gold or timber (Pailes and Reff 1985:356; Tartaron 2005:154); in many other instances they served as emporia or as nodes in a trade diaspora connecting not only with each other but also with the center and more distant areas (Spence 2005:175). Imperialism and colonialism, as Okun (1989:12) points out, are not identical phenomena, but often share many features, including frontier settlements created as an economic periphery established through expansion and the incorporation of new territory, the main difference being the presence, nature and number of settlers.

I will now examine specific processes in terms of traditional economic activities such as acquisition, production, distribution and consumption. I have already discussed acquisition in general terms, particularly in respect to frontiers, where most of this activity occurs. Foremost is the acquisition of land itself, which may be obtained by purchase, exchange or force. The land is then used for a variety of purposes, including settlement, farming, pasturage and mining. Another resource previously discussed is labor, either hired or unfree, i.e., gained through the process of enslavement; slaves in turn are either purchased or taken by force. Similarly, raw materials are acquired either using local labor or bought from or traded with middlemen (e.g., Dyson 1985:274–275; Wells 1992:179).

As noted above, the majority of production took place in the core zone, both for use within the core and for export to the periphery. The most significant form of production of course was agriculture, but also included items made in workshops such as wooden and metal tools, furniture and weapons, textiles, ceramics and jewelry. According to the center/periphery model border regions tended to have a more mixed economy, acting as middlemen and interacting with both the core and frontier regions and thus production would occur primarily in regional or provincial workshops, many of them associated with larger settlements and/or local elites. In frontier zones agricultural production tended to be extensive rather than intensive, often with a focus on pastoralism; this subsistence farming was largely incompatible with that practiced in or imposed from the center (Berkhofer 1981:54). In border zones, and to a lesser extent in frontier zones, increasing demand leads to the promotion of craft production from a part-time to a full-time activity, and to specialization in items desired in the core zone, particularly those requiring considerable skill and/or exotic raw materials (Schortman and Urban 1994:403).

The most studied economic process in peripheries is distribution, particularly in the form of trade or exchange. These processes can be broken down further into gift trade, administered or treaty trade and market trade and reciprocity, redistribution and exchange, respectively (Polanyi et al. 1957; cf. Cunliffe 1988:4–6). Distinctions are often made, as noted earlier, between high-value luxury items—usually, at least in principle, seen as part of elite gift exchange networks—and bulk or staple goods; these categories, though not necessarily mutually exclusive, have sometimes been associated with separate and distinct exchange systems, but arguments have also been made for such items to be shipped together, even over long distances, especially by sea.

Kardulias (1999:62) asserts that there was a tripartite exchange system in the Bronze Age Aegean with internal, intermediate and long-distance components, whereby bulk goods circulated in the first two and prestige goods in the third. Hedeager proposes a similar arrangement for the Roman empire, also with three zones: the Roman empire, with a money and market economy; a buffer zone with a limited money economy and lacking an independent currency; and Free Germany, using money, but without a monetary economy (1979:210; cf. Millett 1990:50; Wells 1992:179). Given such evidence, Wells (1992:185) posits that

> from these examples we might propose a general model. Easy access to goods from another culture—in this case along the frontier—results in their integration into the local everyday milieu and mitigates against their use as objects signifying special status. When imports are not easily accessible, as in the hinterlands far removed from the frontier, then such objects can be adopted by elites for purposes of status display.

The role of long-distance trade in core states has also been debated, with some recent acknowledgement of its centrality in ancient economies (Smith 1998:261).

Much cross-border and/or cross-frontier trade—especially that between nomadic pastoralists and sedentary agriculturalists—was symbiotic, with pastoralists regularly supplying items such as horses, milk products, meat, hide and wool that were in short supply and highly valued in agricultural communities, in exchange for grain, metal products, textiles and luxury items. On the northern Chinese border, where such exchange, with fluctuations, occurred regularly over long periods of time, this trade was usually more necessary and desirable for the nomadic barbarians than the settled Chinese. The Chinese government tended to view trade as a form of political control, and its efforts periodically to restrict or prohibit trade were one of the greatest sources of tension along the frontier (Lattimore 1979:38–39; Szynkiewicz 1989:155–156). Grain in particular was greatly desired by nomadic groups because it could be stored for long periods and complemented milk products and meat; since there was a limit to the distance grain could be shipped overland by the Chinese, this made the barbarian market, with transportation facilitated by the use of camels, highly desirable (Lattimore 1962:487–488; Barfield 2001:18).

The institutionalization of trade reinforced regional redistribution systems, and one consequence of such development was the emergence of gateway communities (Hirth 1978:36).

> Gateway communities develop either as a response to increased trade or to the settling of sparsely populated frontier areas. They generally are located along natural corridors of communication and at the critical passages between areas of high mineral, agricultural, or craft productivity; dense population; high demand or supply for scarce resources; and, at the interface of different technologies or levels of sociopolitical complexity. They often occur along economic shear lines where cost factors change and where there are economic discontinuities in the free movement of merchandise. The function of these settlements is to satisfy demand for commodities through trade and the location of these communities reduces transportation costs involved in their movement [Hirth 1978:36; cf. Cunliffe 1988:4–6; Tartaron 2001, 2004, 2005:154].

Gateway communities are structurally similar to dendritic market networks, which are "characteristic of many primitive economic systems and frequently are found in areas where the population is dispersed, transportation is difficult or underdeveloped, and where there is a strong external economic orientation" (Hirth 1978:37). The second level of the network would be smaller hinterland communities which supplied products to the gateway community and received in turn imported items and materials, serving therefore as foci for trade and residence for the elites controlling the trade (Hirth 1978:38; Wells 1987:146).

A key element in both exchange and redistribution is transportation cost, an obvious consideration in peripheries, where distance proves to be a limiting factor in any number of ways, but perhaps most significantly for economic transactions. Thus, for example, as noted earlier, "under preindustrial conditions, transport costs structure the organization of exchange and tribute so the predominant exchange goods shift from bulk to luxury items once a certain distance threshold is reached" (Stein 1998:229; cf. Hedeager 1979:210). Likewise, "different goods circulate through different mechanisms depending upon the nature of the goods, the social subgroups involved in giving and receiving them, and the distances over which they are carried"; such mechanisms include barter, gift-giving, administered trade, market trade, tribute, ransom, taxes, tolls and plunder (Wells 1980:8). Wells suggests, for example, that in Roman border regions the dominant mode was market trade in cattle, cattle products and other bulk commodities, while gift trade played a more significant role in the transmission of luxury items to frontier elites (1992:185).

In respect to redistribution in the periphery, institutionalization of trade also helped to reinforce regional redistribution systems, because new kinds of items—both subsistence commodities as well as more exotic goods—were added to preexisting networks. As the collection, preparation and movement of goods between regions became more complex, a larger and more sophisticated organization was required to manage these economic activities, particularly with the increasing incorporation of long-distance trade (Hirth 1978:36). This development often took the form of trade administered by and through the office of a chief or member of the elite class, whereby economic interaction was strictly regulated in regard to time, place and conditions. Imported goods were redistributed, with some luxury items distributed to subordinates and other members of the elite class, while less valued goods were distributed more widely to lower-ranking groups and individuals; the majority of the rural population, on the other hand, had limited or minimal interest in or access to any imported items (Wells 1980:92–93; Whittaker 1994:125–129).

In the Roman economic system,

> Luxury goods pass through the intermediate zone, which allows, and possibly facilitates, their passage, receiving in return low-value goods. They are retained in the elite distribution zone where they generate, through processes of reciprocity, commodities for exchange with the procurement zone. The bulk of raw materials and manpower produced in the procurement zone flow down through the system, largely unaltered, to the ports-of-trade [Cunliffe 1988:200].

D'Agata notes that imported goods circulated fairly freely in markets with access to their manufacturers, but imitations arose more easily in peripheral centers where circulation of imported material was fairly limited (2000:64). On the Roman frontier in Germany, approximately one-third of all objects found in settlements—including

4. Border and Frontier Processes

several types of pottery, utilitarian metal objects, bronze and glass serving and drinking vessels, and coins—were imported and were incorporated largely by replacing equivalent indigenous forms (Wells 1992:181).

The focus and coordinator of economic activity in most societies was the leader or headman, functioning as the economic center, collecting, storing, and redistributing goods and services as well coordinating public activities involving group labor and the production of goods (Wells 1980:7–8).

> In a prestige-goods economy, elites—usually male lineage heads— obtain power by controlling access to goods obtainable only through external exchange.... Subordinate individuals become dependent upon lineage heads for access to these valuables. The lineage heads in turn extract surplus production of both utilitarian goods and valuables in return for the provisioning of these social necessities. The lineage heads use this surplus production in status competitions with other lineage heads, and to obtain more valuables from outside the society [McGuire 1989:49].

In Iron Age Europe, for example, central European chieftains, in return for readily obtainable products required or desired by Mediterranean urban centers, acquired first Greek and then Roman luxury goods including wine, fine pottery, sophisticated bronze metalwork and a range of organic materials such as silk, ivory and coral. Eventually the increasing Mediterranean demand for central European products enhanced the economic power of local chiefs, which along with their political power and social status, enabled them to reorganize their own economy in order to produce surpluses to meet this demand, thus initiating a feedback loop in which external trade and economic power increased (Wells 1980:5; Nash 1985:50).

Economic processes are often closely related to social and political processes in peripheries, although rarely in a deterministic manner. For example, similar kinds of exchange may occur within a variety of different political systems (Cunliffe 1988:3), although the complexity and sophistication of such systems will of course influence the specific nature and organization of exchange. Likewise, even in relatively homogeneous environmental and cultural regions, different commercial activity can lead to the formation of different kinds of political units (Wells 1987:141). And although political and economic boundaries may coincide and sometimes separate different economic *and* political systems (Lattimore 1962:481), economic networks such as trade diasporas may function independently of the polities within which they are embedded (Spence 2005:175).

Certainly economic networks—either a peer polity relationship of relative equals or the more asymmetrical core/periphery system—could exceed the size of individual polities and extend well beyond the boundaries of a given state (Kristiansen and Larsen 2005:48; cf. Hirth 1978:37; Dyson 1985:130). And such mutual economic interest between settled and nomadic societies in frontier zones could lead to changes in political allegiance or alliance at times as well (Lattimore 1962:481). Sometimes, too, trading privileges—or their denial—could be used as a political weapon (Whittaker 1994:223).

Spence goes on to point out, however, that although trade represents a significant aspect of such communities, cultural distinctiveness as a matrix for interaction and embodying ethnic roles may supersede economic function (2005:175). Likewise, it has been well established by adherents of the substantivist school that the social context of exchange may loom larger than its economic value and may receive greater public emphasis than financial significance (cf. Wells 1980:144).

Social and Cultural Processes

Social and cultural processes, in my view, represent some of the most interesting kinds of interactions within peripheries. The close proximity of groups—some of which are indigenous, others intrusive—promotes opportunities for culture contact and culture change. I focus here on three related aspects of culture contact and change: acculturation, ethnicity and intermarriage.

Cultural interaction can occur in a wide variety of contexts and involve various agents and processes. Interaction can be neutral, friendly or hostile. It can occur in social, political, economic, and ceremonial contexts, and in many cases may involve more than one of these aspects simultaneously or serially. Contacts between groups of people are shaped or channeled in part by systemic factors—including distance, demography, and power differentials—but are also driven by the collective actions and motivations of hundreds, if not thousands,

4. Border and Frontier Processes

of individuals (Willey et al. 1956; Alexander 1998:478–481; Cusick 1998a:6–7).

Anyone, of course, can in principle interact with someone from another culture, but some individuals and groups are more likely to do so than others: generally, for example, intercultural contact involves males rather than females, adults rather than children and elites rather than commoners, although in some circumstances, such as intermarriage, women and children are perforce participants (Redfield et al. 1935:146; Okun 1989:135–136). Those making initial contact with other cultures (through, for example, exploration, conquest or trade) tend to be different than those who may subsequently do so (by settlement); for instance, during the European colonization of the New World, Asia, and Africa, those first making contact were usually soldiers and missionaries, and sometimes traders. In the great majority of instances culture contact results in some form of change, adjustment or integration.

The typical venue for such encounters represents, in both spatial and social terms, an intermediate contact zone, external to the center of at least one group, i.e., peripheral zones such as borders and frontiers (Cusick 1998a:6–7; Rice 1998; Feuer 2003, 2011). Such places, often characterized as middle ground or a third space, comprise arenas hospitable to the interchange of objects, techniques or concepts. Contact situations are structured but not deterministic, involving processes of social and cultural integration leading to mutual borrowing and the subsequent revision of cultural elements (Spicer 1961:519; White 1991; Cusick 1998a:6–7; Antonaccio 2003:60). One significant variable here is the nature and duration of contact. The potential permutations of such encounters are virtually infinite, ranging from two individuals to entire groups, and from single meetings to daily interaction. Certainly a single contact is unlikely to result in measurable change, while repeated, regular or even daily interaction is likely to result in a wide range of outcomes along a continuum of lesser to greater integration (Willey et al. 1956; Spicer 1961; Herskovits 1967:174; Gosden 2004).

It is on the periphery that one is most likely to encounter the Other (or an Other), to experience and encounter aspects of the Other that seem attractive or appealing, to adopt or appropriate aspects of the Other's culture or even to become the Other (Cusick 1998a:4). The periphery is also the most likely location for ethnogenesis to occur, i.e.,

71

for the processes of syncretization to result in the creation of a new identity (Chappell 1993; Hall 2000:241; Stein 2005:28; Luraghi 2008: 15).

Acculturation

One interaction process studied intensively by anthropologists and archaeologists, and closely related to acculturation, is diffusion, which may be defined as the acceptance of something new or different by individuals or groups linked by specific channels of communication within a sociocultural structure (Katz et al. 1963:240; Schortman and Urban 1987:40–48; Wagner 1988:179–181; Kristiansen and Larsson 2005:25–27). Although diffusion studies have fallen out of fashion, the basic concept, of transmission and reception, is still, in my opinion, valid. Various mechanisms may be involved, although the most common ones are cultural and/or economic (Hugill and Dickson 1988).

The process of diffusion often, but not inevitably, follows a sequence whereby objects of material culture are initially transmitted and/or borrowed, usually by means of exchange, sometimes, but not always, followed by methods, and finally ideas; this sequence is not, however, inevitable and things, practices, and beliefs may also be transmitted simultaneously. Most commonly, individual traits or items are borrowed, but on occasion packages or bundles of related things may be transferred (van der Leeuw 1983:24; Butzer 1988:105). Diffusion can occur as the result of migration or the movement of peoples whereby an entire cultural repertoire or assemblage moves physically to another locale; colonization is the most common form of what is referred to as primary diffusion. In secondary or stimulus diffusion, however, items or ideas can move without face-to-face contact, by means of intermediate parties, such as through down-the-line trade. Trade, especially long-distance exchange, has been considered a significant causal factor in sociopolitical evolution, in addition to the transfer of goods (Schortman and Urban 1987:45–52). At least two phases of transmission usually occur: external diffusion from one culture to another, followed by internal diffusion within a culture (Schortman and Urban 1987; Butzer 1988:106).

Although I have somewhat arbitrarily separated diffusion and acculturation as related aspects of culture contact and change for pur-

4. Border and Frontier Processes

poses of analysis, it should be apparent that in operational terms—and in an archaeological context—they are in fact inextricably intertwined, and it is often difficult to distinguish where diffusion ends and acculturation begins (Herskovits 1967:159–171; van der Leeuw 1983; Kristiansen and Larsson 2005:25–27; cf. Redfield et al. 1935:145–6). Acculturation can be defined as "those phenomena which result when groups of individuals having different cultures come into continuous first-hand contact, with subsequent changes in the original cultural patterns of either or both groups" (Redfield et al. 1935:145–146; cf. Bloemers 1989:78; see also Spicer 1961:517–519; Cusick 1998b; Deagan 1998:26–28). It is "the internal or local process of assimilating foreign cultural traits as a result of diffusion between cultures. In this process the new traits are recontextualised and given meaning" (Kristiansen and Larsson 2005:26–27). It is thus both the processes and the results of culture contact (Foster 1960:7).

Significant parameters of acculturation include: (1) cultural systems and their characteristic features; (2) the conditions under which interaction takes place; and (3) the nature of the relations between the different cultures (Bloemers 1989:178). Situations in which acculturation may occur include: (1) those where elements of culture are forced on a people or are received voluntarily by them; (2) those where there is no social or political inequality between groups; or (3) those where inequality exists between groups, such as political dominance by one group with or without recognition of its social dominance by the subject group (Redfield et al. 1935:146; cf. Gosden 2004:82).

Another way to characterize and differentiate conditions of acculturation is in terms of directed or non-directed change (Linton 1936; Foster 1960; Cusick 1998a:6–7). Directed change—of which there are numerous examples in both the archaeological and historical record— takes the form of colonialism and/or imperialism, whereby change is imposed upon other societies by means of political and/or military control. Not all colonies are established and maintained by means of force, but a substantial proportion of them have employed some form of coercion, including forced acculturation.

Non-directed change, on the other hand, often takes place within a middle ground whereby the inhabitants of the recipient culture are able to exercise choice in the selection of specific aspects of the donor culture (e.g., Antonaccio 2003; Gosden 2004:88–89; Schoep 2006:50;

Hodos 2009, 2010). Under these circumstances the role of consumption and consumer demand, along with other local conditions and dynamics emphasizing the active role of indigenous groups in appropriating foreign elements requires greater attention (Ezell 1961; Dietler 1997:297; 2005:63; Stein 2005:9; Hodos 2006:203). Of course, even in instances of directed change, some members of the recipient society may freely adopt foreign cultural elements, and in situations of non-directed change some people (e.g., family members) may be coerced into adopting foreign items or behavior. In terms of the impact on the recipient culture, this translates into aspects of control, influence, or both in the domains of political, social, economic, religious or cultural activity or behavior. "Control" implies coercion or the threat of force in the acceptance of new or different cultural elements, while "influence" (a commonly employed term in the archaeological literature) suggests room for agency and choice.

Leaving aside the issue of whether any human interaction leaves either or both parties entirely unchanged, we may posit that no discernible alteration may on occasion occur. It is possible, for instance, that a single encounter may not result in any measurable change. However, in most instances, particularly where regular or patterned interaction occurs, the outcome may range along a continuum from no change to radical alteration. At one end of the continuum no borrowing may take place—and thus no change occurs—as the result of lack of interest or active resistance or rejection (Devereux and Loeb 1943). At the other end of the continuum is wholesale transformation, resulting in assimilation or ethnogenesis; in the former case, wholesale adoption of another culture almost always is imposed by force or coercion; in the latter instance a new cultural entity—and identity— emerges from a process of hybridization. The most commonly identified agents of forcible change are most often identified as colonization and/or imperialism.

In between these polar extremes falls partial acculturation, involving the exercise of choice ranging from the acceptance of a single item, trait, method, or idea to substantial borrowing of multiple elements of different kinds, some of which may comprise "packages" of related cultural aspects. The dynamics of acceptance and internal diffusion of single traits is obviously easier and simpler than a complex of things, practices, and concepts, and the need for modification and adjustment

4. Border and Frontier Processes

is necessarily greater in the latter case (van der Leeuw 1983:24; Butzer 1988:105; Okun 1989:135–136; Feuer 2011:518–520).

As the result of diffusion, options for change are presented or made available (Farriss 1983:1–2). Where a middle ground exists the actors exercise agency both in offering cultural elements and in selecting those aspects which are sufficiently appealing to justify the effort of appropriation and whatever adaptation is necessary in order for incorporation (Dietler 1997, 2005; Antonaccio 2003; Gosden 2004; Hodos 2006). The concept of agency assumes some significance here in that the actors are perceived as neither entirely free agents—i.e., they are constrained by local social, political and economic conditions—nor are they wholly powerless drones unable to exercise choice (Díaz-Andreu and Lucy 2005:5; cf. Axelrod 1997). A significant feature of acculturation is that the context and significance of the diffused item inevitably differ in the respective societies. Therefore general-purpose items are often more easily accepted than those which have a limited and specific function. Items whose use is transparent and easily apprehended also tend to be incorporated more readily. In general, things whose utility is easy to ascertain are more likely to be adopted, particularly when they are recognized as meeting a perceived need; thus new techniques or technologies tend to supplement rather than replace elements of the local culture and are adapted and fitted into the existing system (Daniel 1975; van der Leeuw 1983:24; Okun 1989:135–136).

Studies of acculturation indicate that the meaning of things is neither invariable nor inherent in the thing borrowed, but depends upon the nature of the thing borrowed and the contexts of the donor and recipient individuals or groups (van der Leeuw 1983; van Wijngaarden 2001; Wells 2001:25). Moreover, as Axtell notes, "the *way* people of one culture use or adapt another culture's artifacts (ideas, material objects, institutions, language) is more diagnostic of cultural change or acculturation than *what* they adopt" (1981:245–246). Since it is precisely this condition of partial acculturation that can at least potentially occur as the result of interaction between different groups in border or frontier zones, such indeterminacy would seem to comprise a salient feature of such regions.

Differential acculturation can occur in a number of ways. Exposure to new or different ideas or artifacts and opportunity to adopt them would clearly be one such variable. Gender or social class would be other variables influencing acculturation as well. One pattern well attested in ethnohistoric and historic contexts, for example, is the greater tendency of an elite class to welcome or seek acculturation or assimilation into another culture than other elements of a society, often in competition with other similar groups for political power, economic benefits and/or social status, a process referred to as emulation (e.g., Melas 1988; Brass 1991:26; Lightfoot and Martinez 1995:486; Woolf 1998:14–16; Sherratt 1999:174–176; Stein 1999:66–67; Higginbotham 2000; Broodbank 2004:58). The processes of creolization, hybridism or syncretism, for example, in which an amalgam of cultural traits is fused into a synthesis resembling but different than the donor cultures, may represent a strategy of emergent elites to distinguish themselves from other cultural, social or political elements (Tambs-Lyche 1994:69; Stein 2005:28; but cf. Webster 2001; Luraghi 2008; Marotta 2008), and may, over time, result in ethnogenesis, the creation of a new cultural or ethnic identity (Rosman and Rubel 1998:320–322).

Just as those who are responsible for diffusing cultural elements are not necessarily representative of an entire group, those who choose or select them for incorporation are usually subgroups of the whole as well. Any society is comprised of those who generally resist change, those who are attracted to innovation and a large proportion who accept change, but are not in the vanguard of doing so. In stratified societies, members of emerging or existing elites seem particularly receptive to innovations which might legitimize, enhance, or maintain their prestige, wealth or power (Millett 1970; Bartel 1980:18; Leventhal et al. 1987:180; Schortman and Urban 1998:111; Smith 1998). As a result, elites and urban populations tend to be the first to adopt innovations and become more quickly and thoroughly acculturated than the lower classes and rural populations (Okun 1989:135–136).

Such acquisitions are then displayed and manipulated in public contexts such as weddings, burials or other ceremonial occasions and signal status and identity to various constituencies, including the local community and other elites with whom they are both trading and competing (Wells 1992:185–186; Okun 1989:135–136; Kurchin 1995:128). Public feasting, for example, seems to have been a frequent occasion for the conspicuous use of imported items and practices such as exotic foods, eating and drinking vessels and utensils, and ceremonial activities (Dietler 1997, 1998; Davis and Bennet 1999; Vianello 2005; Galaty

76

4. Border and Frontier Processes

and Parkinson 2007; Vives-Ferrándiz 2008:264; Mac Sweeney 2009). This "commensal hospitality" "becomes a key element in establishing relations of reciprocal obligation that bind together host and guest. Drinking also has a common function of promoting social solidarity through its institutionalized role in the context of formal community social rituals, such as festivals and religious rites" (Dietler 1998:302).

One aspect which I have studied somewhat extensively is acculturation's effect on the creation and maintenance of cultural identity (Feuer 2011; cf. Vives-Ferrándiz 2008; Mac Sweeney 2009). Adherence to cultural or ethnic identity is certainly one of the variables which affects the decision to adopt foreign cultural elements. Likewise, any change in material culture, social practices or beliefs will of necessity— whether consciously or not—modify personal or class identity. If an entire society—or even a large proportion of it—accepts a relatively small number of things from other cultures, its cultural identity may shift a bit (because, in fact, societies are never completely static), but this is unlikely to influence how that identity is perceived. However, if or when a substantial portion of a society incorporates external elements, leading to a hybrid culture, or if two groups exchange a significant number of cultural elements, then a new cultural identity begins to emerge which if carried far enough leads to ethnogenesis, the creation of a distinct cultural or ethnic identity (Deagan 1998:29–30; Rossman and Rubel 1998:320–322; Smith 1998:258; Voskos and Knapp 2008). Similarly, if the process of assimilation is sufficiently thorough, the original identity of a group may be lost and replaced by the adopted identity (Ezell 1961; van der Leeuw 1983; Okun 1989).

In summary,

acculturation is a mutual process that affects each culture somewhat differently. The differences derive essentially from the nature of the cultures that meet and the conditions of contact. Cultures can be relatively open and flexible or closed and rigid, depending on such variables as their capacity for corporate definition, size, social integration, kinship and settlement patterns, and attitudes toward, distance from, and relative power vis-a-vis strangers. They can also be aggressive, intent upon directing or inducing change in the cultures they meet, or largely defensive, willing to tolerate other cultures in return for the freedom to determine their own cultural imperatives and strategies. Whatever their natures, the outcome of contact also depends upon the historical time, demographical space, and geographical place in which the cultures meet. The changes that result from this contact vary from microscopic introductions of cultural materials and traits—new cultural contents—to macroscopic alterations of fundamental structures and patterns—new cultural forms for integrating and assimilating foreign elements [Axtell 1981:247].

It should be clear from this brief overview that acculturation is a complex process with many variables and multiple outcomes.

Ethnicity

Ethnicity can be viewed as one of a number of dimensions along which humans can be subdivided into groups, analogous to those formed on the basis of social rank, wealth, or occupational specialization (Gerstle 1984:328; Hutchinson and Smith 1996:3; Wells 1998:317; Siapkas 2003:12). Most if not all of them speak to one of the most basic and profound questions of human existence: who am I—as well as who are they? Like other dimensions which result in the assignment of individuals to a subset of a larger population, ethnicity comprises all of the social and psychological phenomena associated with a culturally constructed group identity, focusing on ways in which social and cultural processes intersect with one another in the identification of and interaction between ethnic groups (Jones 1997; Ostergard 1992:36–37). Reckoning of ethnicity derives from the cultural interpretation of descent, based upon the tendency of human beings to select positively in favor of kin, and so shares many of the same emotional ties as kinship (Keyes 1981:5–7). It is the condition wherein certain members of a society in a given social context choose to emphasize as their most meaningful basis of primary extrafamilial identity certain assumed cultural, national or somatic traits (Patterson 1975:308). And it is the belief in shared ancestry which creates group cohesion (Amory 1997:xiv).

An ethnic group is comprised of people who set themselves apart and/or are set apart by others with whom they interact or coexist on the basis of their perceptions of cultural differentiation and/or common descent and shared culture (Jones 1997:xiii; Fenton 2003:3; Siapkas 2003:15). Such a group is largely biologically self-perpetuating, makes up a field of communication and interaction, and has a membership which identifies itself and is identified by others as constituting a cat-

4. Border and Frontier Processes

egory distinguishable from other categories of the same order (Barth 1969:10–11). Ethnic groups may be mutually exclusive, but

> since descent can be posited with different "ancestors" who lived at different times in the past and can be traced through either or both parents, it is possible for a person to belong to more than one ethnic group just as he or she might belong to more than one descent-defined kin group [Keyes 1981:6].

Although modern studies of ethnicity often emphasize ethnic minorities within larger political entities, ethnic groups can in fact range from small, relatively isolated kin groups to larger categories of people defined as alike on the basis of a limited number of characteristics (Yinger 1985:157).

Ethnic identity thus represents that aspect of a person's self-conceptualization which results from identification with a broader group in opposition to others on the basis of perceived cultural differences (Jones 1997:xiii), i.e., an individual's allegiance to a community as manifested in behavioral and cultural traits (Amory 1997:xiv) involving the subjective, symbolic or emblematic use of any aspect of a culture or a perceived separate origin and continuity in order to differentiate him/herself from those in other groups (De Vos 1995:24). Ethnic identity includes the recognition among members of a common history and purpose, the sharing of common assumptions for generating and evaluating appropriate behavior, recognition of the validity of the status of others with whom the members interact, and symbolic expression of status through display of physical markers of membership (Hutchinson and Smith 1996:4–7; Schortman and Urban 1987:64).

An ethnic group can be considered a type of descent group whose members validate their claim to shared descent by pointing to cultural attributes which they believe they hold in common, and unlike races, are not thought of as mutually exclusive, but are structured in segmentary hierarchies (Keyes 1981:5–6; cf. De Vos 1995:18–19). Patterson makes the following distinctions between cultural groups and ethnic groups: (1) while a cultural group is simply any group of people who consciously or unconsciously share an identifiable complex of meanings, symbols, values, and norms, an ethnic group maintains a conscious awareness of belonging by members and a conscious group identity; (2) a cultural group is an objectively verifiable social phenomenon whose traditions can be anthropologically observed, regardless of the ideological statements, or expressed opinions, of members about their tradition or their relationship with it; (3) a cultural group, or segments of it, may become an ethnic group, but only when the conditions of ethnicity are met. If a segment of a cultural group identifies or designates itself as an ethnic group, this does not mean that all members of the cultural group thereby become an ethnic group (1975:309–310; cf. Zenner, 1978:328; Linnekin and Poyer 1990:1–2). Finally, as Chappell notes, "Whereas cultures are complex and relatively open ... ethnicity stresses boundary formation based on rather more simplistic criteria" (1993:268).

One widely-discussed issue is whether ethnicity is essentially primordial or instrumental (Nagata 1981:89; Linnekin and Poyer 1990:2–4; Eller and Coughlan 1993; Grosby 1994; Hutchinson and Smith 1996:8–9; Hall 1997:17–19; Monroe 2002:12–13; Fenton 2003:73–90; Siapkas 2003:207). The primordialist theory holds that ethnicity emanates from a corpus of basic, elemental and irreducible loyalties (Jones 1997:65–72; Nagata 1981:89). According to Jones, primordial theories of ethnicity result in a romanticization and mystification of ethnic identity, suggesting that ethnic identity is a determining and immutable dimension of an individual's self-identity because the primordial attachments that underlie ethnicity are involuntary and coercive; thus ethnicity becomes an abstract natural phenomenon which can be explained on the basis of "human nature" (1997:68–70; cf. Howard 1990; Siapkas 2003:170; Luraghi 2008:6).

The instrumental approach, on the other hand, focuses on ethnicity as a dependent variable, created and controlled by a broad combination of external interests and strategies investing it with a potential for action and mobilization (Nagata 1981:89; Siapkas 2003:281). This perspective emphasizes ethnicity as a socially or culturally constructed category (e.g., Siapkas 2003:175–176). Those holding this view may fall into a reductionist mode of explanation whereby ethnicity is defined in terms of the observed regularities of ethnic behavior in a particular situation, and the reduction of ethnicity to economic and political relationships frequently results in a neglect of the cultural dimensions of ethnicity, a consequence of the idea that ethnic categories provide an empty vessel into which various aspects of culture can be poured; unlike the primordialist position which emphasizes the emotional and irrational aspects of ethnic identity, the instrumentalist perspective assumes that human behavior is essentially rational and directed toward maximizing self-interest (Jones 1997:76–79).

Ethnic identity is created and maintained through the application of ethnic markers or diacritics, which represent claimed points of difference between groups insofar as they are recognized and emphasized by members of the group concerned (Watson 1990:22). Such markers are viewed as intrinsic elements of a group's heritage and constitute a system of classification used to distinguish different categories of people (Keyes 1981:7). As such they serve multiple functions, including identifying and excluding outsiders, enhancing internal solidarity, emphasizing a common heritage, publicly validating the incorporation and assimilation of outsiders, and in some cases justifying autonomy or sovereignty (Brass 1980: 62–63; Galaty 1993:178; Smith 1986:49).

Virtually any aspect of human physiology or culture can function as an ethnic marker, including physical appearance, language, religion, values, customs, traditions and almost any element of material culture (Cohen 1978; Brass 1980:2; Adams 1981:8–13; Gerstle 1984:328–329; Nash 1989:10–15; Renfrew 1996:130; Gosselain 2000:189). Usually, however, only a limited number of a much wider array of potential diacritics is actually so employed (Barth 1969:14; Schortman and Urban 1987:65). Although some markers, such as language, religion, and territory, are frequently used to distinguish among and categorize groups (Cohen 1978:386), no single marker or set of markers is invariably used for this purpose (Moerman 1965:1221).

Though it might be possible to rank specific markers hierarchically in terms of their salience (e.g., Buchignani 1987:20), and though some markers are more commonly employed or more salient than others, ultimately "the choice of which of an almost infinite variety of potential markers to use is arbitrary and unpredictable" (Schortman and Urban 1987:65; cf. Luraghi 2008:9). As Barth notes,

> ethnic categories provide an organizational vessel that may be given varying amounts and forms of content in different sociocultural systems; they may be of great relevance to behavior, but they need not be; they may pervade all social life or they may be relevant only in limited sectors of activity [1969:14].

Clearly, then, considerable variability exists in the choice and use of ethnic markers, and not only does the choice of markers vary among ethnic groups, but different markers may be applied in different contexts, and the number, kind and meaning of markers may change over time (Brass 1980:2; Enloe 1980:350; Buchignani 1987:20; Watson 1990). According to Sandstrom (1991:67),

> Ethnicity is often situational in that people decide when and how to assert their identity using different strategies at different times. An added complicating factor is that over time a group's self-definition changes to meet new challenges, and the symbols people choose to represent their identity may be modified, created anew, intentionally eliminated, or resurrected from a previous period. Thus, any listing of traits poses the danger of oversimplifying and thereby falsifying a complex and constantly shifting multiethnic situation.

So although various markers can assume a primordial role, the recent emphasis on choice and variability by many researchers tends to reinforce the instrumental interpretation of ethnicity.

Ethnic identity may be asserted and used differently in different contexts. Cohen characterizes ethnicity as a series of nesting dichotomizations of inclusiveness and exclusiveness, whereby the process of assigning persons to groups depends upon which diacritics are used to define membership; the greater the number of diacritical markers, the closer one gets to a particular person or group. Those which take in the largest number of people are used at the most inclusive levels of scale, while those that distinguish at lower-scale levels become more important when more localized or smaller-scale distinctions are being made (1978:397; cf. Horowitz 1975:118).

Compared to diacritics such as language, religion and ideology, the relationship of material culture to ethnicity is somewhat more problematic (e.g., Jones 1997:124). It is clear that aspects of material culture such as architecture, dress, and artifacts such as pottery, weapons and jewelry, and even the style of such artifacts, can function as ethnic markers. Yet material culture in and of itself rarely is sufficient to distinguish ethnic groups (DeCorse 1989; Hill 1989:240). Moreover, the effects of choice, contingency and variability make it quite difficult to infer or predict which aspects of material culture in a given situation will be considered more salient. In other words, the salience of ethnic markers cannot be inferred *a priori*, but must be inductively perceived in a given context (Jones 1996:72–73).

The decoration of functional objects or non-utilitarian artifacts,

4. Border and Frontier Processes

as Hodder's ethnoarchaeological analysis in Kenya indicates, can not only reflect or express ethnic identity, but also actively signal or advertise it (1982:57–58; cf. Wobst 1977). Thus differences in material culture may constitute ethnic differences as well as indicate them, enabling members of an ethnic group to mobilize them for the purposes of mutual support, group solidarity or negative reciprocity (Hodder 1982:27; Franklin 1989). Jones (1997:120) concurs:

> Material culture is frequently implicated in both the recognition and expression of ethnicity; it both contributes to the formulation of ethnicity and is structured by it. Certain aspects of material culture may become involved in the self-conscious signification of identity, and the justification and negotiation of ethnic relations. As a result, distinctive forms and styles of material culture may be actively maintained and withheld in the process of signaling ethnicity, whilst other forms and styles may cross-cut ethnic boundaries.

The use and manipulation of ethnic markers create ethnic boundaries between individuals and groups. To speak of an ethnic group, then, is to imply a boundary of some kind which in symbolic form expresses the relationship between ethnic groups (Helms 1988: 28; Spencer 1979:195). As such, ethnic boundaries are a fundamental reality of social organization which have a major effect on the social, political and economic options open to individuals (McGuire 1982:160). However, identifying and defining such boundaries is by no means a straightforward exercise (Creamer 1984:362; Macbeth 1993:74; MacEachern 1998). In most studies of ethnicity, ethnic boundaries are viewed primarily as social boundaries and hence conceptual in nature rather than necessarily physical ones (Ross 1975; Wallman 1978:205; Spencer 1979:205; Eriksen 1991:128; Dolukhanov 1994:29; Hegmon 1998:271–274). Ethnic boundaries can have a territorial manifestation as well, though physical and conceptual boundaries are not isometric and may not therefore necessarily coincide (Banks 1966:14; Barth 1969:15).

Again emphasizing ethnicity as primarily instrumental rather than primordial, Barth also holds that ethnic boundaries persist because of, rather than despite, interaction between ethnic groups (cf. Chappell 1993:268). That is, ethnic boundaries do not necessarily prevent interaction, but instead exist and are maintained *through* interaction; in this sense they may be said both to reflect ethnic identity and to channel

83

social interaction (Barth 1969:10–15; du Toit 1978:9; Hodder 1982; McGuire 1982:160; Sandstrom 1991:71). Because the choice and application of ethnic markers is variable and may change over time or according to context, ethnic boundaries can for the most part be characterized as fluid and flexible (du Toit 1978:9; Spencer 1979:195) or as semi-permeable membranes (Guillotte 1978:20). Therefore, economic processes such as trade could occur or people could be exchanged without affecting the essential nature of the boundary (Barth 1969; Hodder 1982; Spencer 1979:197; Waller 1993:228).

Ethnic boundaries therefore can be seen to arise or be created as part of the process of ethnogenesis, the formation of an ethnic group, based upon whatever markers are deemed significant, and are maintained, negotiated, reinforced, or modified by the application and/or manipulation of such diacritics (Barth 1969:15; Hall 1997:29; Keyes 1981:91; Luraghi 2008:198–208). Conversely, ethnic boundaries may disappear as the result of acculturation, creolization, or assimilation (Goudriaan 1988:12, 1992; Tambs-Lyche 1994; McGuire 1982).

Ethnic boundaries should be indicated by the distribution of ethnic markers (e.g., Wonderly 1986:331; but cf. Creamer 1984:362). If there is any significant correlation of social or conceptual boundaries with an equivalent territorial expression, there should be a decline in frequency of markers at the boundary, or just beyond the boundary, between groups. If such boundaries are relatively impermeable, the decline should be fairly abrupt (Buchignani 1987:21). If, however, boundaries are more or less permeable or if there is the kind of acculturation—either unilateral or mutual—typically associated with border regions, then the fall-off should be more gradual. For example, the attraction of exotic or prestigious beliefs, practices or artifacts should be reflected in their disproportionate presence in such contexts.

It is well established that even within a core zone archaeological assemblages are neither identical nor uniform, but vary according to factors such as age, gender and class. Nevertheless, assuming that an archaeological culture or ethnic group can be identified on the basis of some kind of polythetic model (e.g., Clarke 1978), there should be a core assemblage comprised of ethnic markers that forms the basis of association and defines the group on the basis of its material culture. In peripheral zones, however, this core assemblage can on the one hand

4. Border and Frontier Processes

become attenuated if some of its elements are not present and can on the other hand reflect partial acculturation of other ethnic groups. Moreover, such attenuation and mixing should to some extent represent a function of distance and decreasing integration, so that they should increase from core zone to border zone to frontier zone. In other words, we should expect to find in border and frontier zones mixed assemblages of two or more cultures or ethnic groups (Gerstle 1984:329), and it is such mixed assemblages that I wish to discuss in some detail in respect to the manifestation of ethnic identity in peripheral regions.

The primary archaeological evidence of ethnicity in almost all cases comes from material culture. Though surely not the only—and not necessarily the most important—kind of ethnic marker, material culture can nevertheless be informative about ethnicity and ethnic processes in and of itself (McGuire 1982:163; Luraghi 2008:135–136). The patterning of material culture in the archaeological record can reflect a variety of functions and relationships, of which ethnicity is only one, including economic adaptation, culture, class, gender, and others. Such patterns often overlap because the human beings who make and use items of material culture inhabit multiple realms of identity and activity, some of them simultaneously (Wells 1980, 1992, 2001:21–22; Lightfoot and Martinez 1995:480–483).

One aspect of material culture which has been widely discussed in this respect is style (Wobst 1977; Hodder 1979, 1982; Franklin 1989; Wiessner 1989; Jones 1997:110–122; Sackett 1990; Stahl 1991; Dietler and Herbich 1998; Hegmon 1998; Monroe 2002). As an ethnic marker it has often been used to identify and delineate cultural, ethnic and social boundaries (Ericson and Meighan 1984; Sampson 1988:16; Parkinson 2006; cf. MacEachern 1998). This emblematic usage involving the assertive, active signaling of identity (Hodder 1982; Franklin 1989:279–282; Wiessner 1989) should be distinguished from what Sackett termed isochrestic style, i.e., stylistic variation within a group (1990; cf. Jones 1997:122; Shennan 1989:19). It has also been demonstrated that this kind of signaling becomes more emphatic during periods of crisis or stress, thus sharpening ethnic distinctions (Hodder 1979; Sampson 1988:16; Jones 1997:122; Monroe 2002: 17, 24). Parkinson suggests that the relative visibility and the social and geographical distribution of stylistic artifacts may prove helpful in determining the role a specific attribute may have played within a particular social context (2006:36).

One final dimension of material culture—though often overlooked in this respect—that seems particularly susceptible to analysis is food and food preparation, since certain foods, their method of preparation and the artifacts used to prepare and serve them, seem to be strongly implicated in ethnic identity (Branigan 1984:50; McKee 1987; Borgna 1997; Broodbank 2004:59–60). Archaeological evidence for this behavior includes food remains themselves, artifacts used in the processing and preparation of food, and spaces within structures used for food consumption, particularly ceremonial feasting (King 1984; Deagan 1985:81–82; Garcia-Arevalo 1989:277). In regard to the latter, assemblages associated with these activities, such as drinking sets, found in the archaeological record have been identified as indicative of elite emulation (Sherratt 1999:174–176; Stein 1999:66–67; Kiriatzi 2000; Andreou 2001; Wright 2004).

If, ultimately, the creation and maintenance of ethnic boundaries divides the conceptual, social, and physical environment into Us and Them, then ethnic identity cannot exist without the presence of and interaction with the Other (Helms 1988; Blake 1999; Wells 2001:22; Graner and Karlenby 2007:150, 161–162). Or to put it differently, without the Other, there is no need to assert one's ethnicity. In addition to simple differentiation—i.e., "We are X and they are Y" or "We do things differently"—perception and characterization of the Other almost always involves some degree of ethnocentrism. Thus part of the ethnic boundary process usually involves various ethnic stereotypes and the drawing of distinctions between Us and Them (e.g., Coles and Wolf 1974:272; Guillotte 1978:31; Hodder 1982:27; Helms 1988:51; Theodossopoulos 2003). While one may encounter the Other in a variety of contexts—including within oneself—I emphasize here interactions which take place within border and frontier regions. One of the most common forms of ethnic and cultural distinction made in these contexts—often, but not always, between societies of differing sociocultural complexity (Ferguson and Whitehead 1992; Triulzi 1994:236; Lightfoot and Martinez 1995:473; Tiruchelvam 1996; Wells 2001:22, 108)—is the dichotomy between civilization and barbarism.

In border and frontier zones, therefore, two seemingly contradictory processes occur, characterized by Lattimore as "frontier pressure"

4. Border and Frontier Processes

and "frontier pull" (1962; cf. Whittaker 1994:121–122; Woolf 1998:19). On the one hand ethnic (and other) boundaries serve to limit interaction and to preserve the integrity of cultural and ethnic identity. On the other hand, the attraction of other groups and the desirable results of interaction draw them, or individuals from them, together (Strassoldo 1980:49). One example of a peripheral zone and the processes which occur therein is the United States-Mexican border. Here a border culture of mixed American-Mexican ethnicity is divided by a political boundary which is highly permeable despite the efforts of the American government to make it less so. Considerable trade, human traffic and occasional conflicts take place across the boundary. Despite ethnic markers including language and food, there is ample mutual acculturation, although because of the economic imbalance between the two countries, migration, acculturation and assimilation are much more extensive on the American side of the boundary than on the Mexican side (Price 1973).

In sum, then, it is on the periphery that one is most likely to encounter the Other (or an Other), to experience and encounter aspects of the Other that seem attractive or appealing, to adopt or appropriate aspects of the Other's culture or even to become the Other. The periphery is also the most likely location for ethnogenesis to occur, i.e., for the processes of syncretization to result in the creation of a new identity (Chappell 1993; Deagan 1998:29–30; Hall 2000:241; Stein 2005:28; Luraghi 2008: 15). Interaction involving both ethnicity and peripheral zones is inherently dyadic and fully to understand such interaction therefore necessitates a dual perspective. In other words, one must view such interaction from both sides of the boundary separating the actors. As noted, ethnic processes always involve, either directly or indirectly, the Other; since every Us/Them dichotomy is reversible, in addition to understanding how we view the Other, we need also to consider how the Other views us. Likewise, a spatial boundary divides, no matter how precisely, one border zone from another (or a frontier), so that the boundary and what lies beyond the boundary can and should be seen from both sides (Lightfoot and Martinez 1995; Ross 1975:55).

Of the various processes involving interaction within peripheral areas, most involve ethnicity to some degree and some directly involve ethnic markers and boundaries. One common form of interaction is trade or exchange. Though for the most part ethnic identity is not greatly influenced by such economic transactions, articles of material culture which may function, among other things, as ethnic markers may be exchanged and in some instances may be considered desirable because of this feature. It may also be, as suggested above, that when exchange takes place between members of different ethnic groups that negative reciprocity may be involved. In addition, as Stein (1999:48–49, 2002:31–32) points out, trade diasporas relied on the creation and maintenance of ethnic boundaries in order to assure their continued existence and autonomy.

Moreover, as noted earlier, not all elements of culture are ethnic markers, so the borrowing or adoption of some ideas, practices or items of material culture may not affect the perception of ethnic identity (Tambs-Lyche 1994:61). In respect to ethnic markers, however, it remains to be determined if there is a threshold of acceptability or recognition of ethnic identity. Tweddell, for example, introduces the concept of the "balk line," the point at which one or more groups refuse or decline to adapt or adjust their culture any further (1987:312). If there is a hierarchy of ethnic markers, which ones would cross ethnic boundaries and which would not? Is there a "package" or assemblage of diacritics that signify ethnic identity? In other words, while it is clear that those who possess all of the necessary criteria for belonging to an ethnic group by ascription or who acquire those criteria through assimilation are members of that group, there is an intermediate condition of partial acculturation which would seemingly make ethnic group membership more problematical. Since it is precisely this condition of partial acculturation that can at least potentially occur as the result of interaction between different groups in border or frontier zones, such indeterminacy would seem to comprise a salient feature of such regions.

Intermarriage

In addition to exchange, one of the primary means of acculturation or assimilation is intermarriage, and it has been noted that one thing that typically crosses boundaries—ethnic or otherwise—is people (Abruzzi 1982; Deagan 1985:289, 305–306; Harrell 1990:532–533, 1995:107). In patrilineal and patrilocal societies, for example, men remain within the group and women marry out, going to live with the families of their husbands. Although most exogamous marriages take place between clans or lineages within a culture or ethnic group, sometimes the boundary crossed is cultural or ethnic (Coldstream 1993; Enloe 1980: 354; Ericson and Meighan 1984:145; Galaty 1993:184). This is much more likely to be the case in peripheral zones where contact and interaction between ethnic groups occurs much more frequently. Inevitably in such circumstances the woman adopts the culture, if not the ethnicity, of her husband's family, and her children will very likely belong to that group as well. It is also the case, however, that the wife brings her culture and ethnicity with her, and there is the potential, therefore, however limited, for her to transmit aspects of that culture or ethnicity to others, especially her children. And as Anderton (1986:242) points out, intermarriage is a principal cause and indicator of assimilation.

It would seem reasonable that opportunities for intermarriage would be greater in some circumstances than others, such as in colonial enclaves where the number of non-native women would be limited (Branigan 1981:26; Deagan 1985:81; Coldstream 1993:97; cf. Spence 2005:177), or where the demographic composition of foreigners is primarily or entirely male, such as in military garrisons. Forbes (1968:211; cf. Ericson and Meighan 1984:145; van Dommelen 2006:137) notes that intermarriage, along with acculturation, has been a significant factor in blurring cultural affiliations in peripheries, a process involved in the transformation of borders into extensions of the core zone, and frontiers into borders. In addition to acculturation, intermarriage may also result in the blending of cultural traditions and practices (Deagan 1983; Coldstream 1993:96) and the creation of hybrid cultures.

5

Case Studies

To this point we have looked at boundaries, borders and frontiers largely from a topical, somewhat abstract perspective, with illustrative examples from various periods and cultures. To conclude this discussion of peripheries, I will describe and discuss two examples of societies which exemplify those topics and which have been most thoroughly studied in respect to them. These are two great civilizations, in different parts of the world, and from somewhat different though overlapping time periods. Finally, I will discuss in somewhat greater detail the area in the past with which I am most familiar, Late Bronze Age Thessaly, in order to apply many of the concepts discussed previously to a specific place and time.

China

China is one of the world's oldest civilizations and arguably the longest-lived civilization as well, and as a result, Chinese history and prehistory have been extensively documented and studied, most notably by Owen Lattimore (1962), in respect to boundaries and frontiers. Moreover, the geography of China and eastern Asia influenced long-term patterns of growth, development and interaction which exemplify many of the processes and structures discussed earlier (Figure 4).

The heartland of Chinese culture and civilization is the Huang Ho valley in what is now northern China, a well-watered region with easily-worked and fertile loess soil which was the locus of China's earliest Neolithic societies; this geographical focus can be traced back at least as far as the Yang-shao culture (Szynkiewicz 1989:153). Shang civiliza-

5. Case Studies

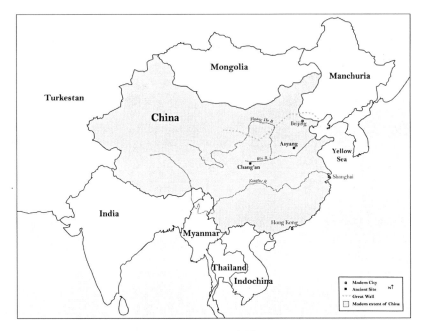

Figure 4: Map of China

tion, the first well-attested state society, also emerged in the Huang Ho valley. With its capital at Anyang, the center of Shang civilization was the valley of the Wei River, a tributary of the Huang Ho; from there, the Shang expanded through much of the central Huang Ho valley, with a periphery of cultural influence beyond their area of political control. Other states emerged within this periphery, and after the collapse of Shang civilization c. 1100 BC, an extensive period of peer polity interaction among these states known as the Warring States period ensued. This inter-state warfare eventually reduced the number of competitors to several large and powerful polities which continued to wage war upon each other until one state, Ch'in, was able to conquer its rivals and create the first Chinese empire in 221 BC.

The center of the Ch'in state was also the Wei River valley, which was located in the area of potential optimal expansion to the north (Lattimore 1962:107). After consolidating its territory, the empire began to expand beyond its core zone in the Huang Ho valley. To the north, the Chinese began to encounter the Mongolian steppes, an environment unsuitable for the intensive wheat and millet cultivation adapted to the loess soil of the core zone; to the south, they moved into the Yangtze valley, an environment most suitable for the growing of rice. Thus, to the north,

> the steppe, as such, demanded of any Chinese who entered it a social modification divergent from the main trend of Chinese development, with the result that the Chinese of the Frontier were fated to vacillate, for twenty centuries and more, between orientation toward the tribal power of the steppe and orientation toward the agriculturally based, dynastic-imperial civilization of China itself [Lattimore 1962:107].

Moreover, the steppe could not be cultivated in the same manner as in the core zone, resulting in a more extensive form of agriculture, less density of settlement and more widely separated settlements (Lattimore 1979:36–37). As Lattimore explains, the Chinese first expanded into other areas of loess soil, the most desirable environment for the intensive growing of millet and wheat, then into increasingly more marginal ecological zones, until reaching the plains of the Mongolian steppe which were more suitable for herding than agriculture. This way of life and its cultural correlates became more and more foreign the farther it impinged on the steppe ecology, and the tribal societies which inhabited it were increasingly more difficult to integrate into the Chinese state (Lattimore 1962:475).

> First there is a zone in which the farmer must give up irrigation and take his chances with the rainfall; the hazard is not so much the low average rainfall as the seasonal irregularity of the rain. The farmer must be content with a much lower yield per acre, which in turn means larger holdings, which again means more widely dispersed settlement. North of this there is a zone in which a mixed economy is much safer than reliance on cultivation alone; if enough of the land is reserved for livestock there will usually be enough rain for the pasture when there is not enough for a given crop. Finally there is a zone where herding is the only rational economy; though even here there are patches where if the crop matures it is a gain, while if it fails no serious harm is done [Lattimore 1962:466–467; cf. Boardman 1965:97–98].

This led to the creation of a zone separating the Chinese core from the barbarian border and frontier. Peoples who could not or would not be assimilated were pushed into and beyond this zone into the steppe, where they maintained or adopted a pastoral nomadic existence. This zone, which eventually was established and defined by one of the most

5. Case Studies

substantial boundaries ever constructed, the Great Wall, thus marked the limit of normal Chinese expansion and represented an effort to prevent incursions from the north (Lattimore 1962:110, 477). Beyond the Great Wall a similar process of consolidation was taking place among the nomadic tribes of the steppe, resulting in a unified nomadic empire which opposed and challenged the Chinese empire (Lattimore 1980:207; cf. Barfield 1989:7). To the east and west of these empires were, respectively, Turkestan and Manchuria, characterized by mixed economies rather than the wholly agricultural core and the wholly pastoral frontier; when these empires were strong, the adjoining peripheries fell under the control of one or the other, but during periods when centralized control slackened, they became autonomous states (Barfield 1989:16–18).

A cyclical process of interaction, of successive phases of expansion and withdrawal from both sides of the Great Wall, thus ensued over the course of almost two millennia. Lattimore terms this process one of frontier pull—whereby the Chinese were drawn further into the steppe frontier—and frontier push or pressure from the Hsiung Nu and other barbarian nomadic pastoralists (1962:107, 211; cf. Barfield 1989:10–15). If the Chinese moved too far into the steppe zone they ran the risk of assimilation into tribalism and pastoral nomadism; if the nomads penetrated too far into the Chinese core zone, they likewise had to counter the forces of assimilation and sinicization (Lattimore 1962:114; cf. Barfield 1989:100). Between the extreme poles of core sedentism and frontier pastoralism lay the borderland, termed by Lattimore an inner and outer reservoir, a semi-periphery comprised of

a graduated series of social groups, from partly sinicized nomads and semibarbarized Chinese, in the zone adjacent to China, to steppe peoples in Mongolia, forest peoples in North Manchuria and Urianghai, and peoples of the plateau in Tibet, of whom the more distant were virtually unmodified by such attenuated contacts as they had with China [Lattimore 1962:115].

However, it was not necessary for the nomads to invade the area south of the Great Wall in order to gain favorable treatment from the imperial Chinese government; merely the threat of violent incursion was often sufficient to extract a guarantee of favorable treatment. The alternation of quick violent raiding with equally rapid withdrawal created a sense of anxiety and insecurity at the Chinese court, whose options to respond to such threats were limited, and all of which were expensive: fortify the Great Wall further and ignore demands for tribute or favorable treatment; raise an army and invade the steppes; or sign peace treaties granting economic advantages (Lattimore 1962:484–485; Boardman 1965:99; Barfield 1989:9, 2001:16). Since trade was more important to the nomadic barbarians than the Chinese, the Chinese could also attempt to gain leverage by threatening to withhold trade relations (Szynkiewicz 1989:155–156).

To the south, on the other hand, toward the Yangtze valley, virtually unlimited expansion could take place by means of cellular growth, whereby territorial units could be added by incorporating them into the intensive agricultural regime established in the Huang Ho valley. Although the cultivation of rice made somewhat different demands than that of wheat and millet, the population could nonetheless be incorporated into the existing econo-sociopolitical structure of peasants, landed gentry and government bureaucrats and local exchange networks (Lattimore 1962:104, 476, 481). There were no natural barriers to expansion, new blocks of territory could be added gradually, and the indigenous peoples were already becoming agricultural or were being influenced in that direction by contact with more advanced societies in south Asia. As in the north, the most arable plains and valleys were acquired first, then more marginal areas, isolating less developed tribes in hillier and more mountainous terrain (Lattimore 1962:475).

The ecological contrast between the northern and southern peripheries of the core zone combined with "the social commitment of the Chinese to a specialized complex of agricultural practices and administrative organization" (Lattimore 1962:476) thus led to the creation of two different kinds of frontier. The northern periphery can be described as a static frontier of exclusion, and the southern periphery a dynamic frontier of inclusion (Lattimore 1962:477, 1980:206; cf. Barfield 1989:18).

Given the exigencies involved in establishing and maintaining these peripheries, particularly after the emergence of the empire in the 2nd century BC, it is perhaps not surprising that the imperial bureaucracy developed a distinctive perspective and frontier policy in order to manage its increasingly diverse and far-flung borders and frontiers. Increasingly, the imperial court viewed itself and the Chinese core zone as the "middle kingdom," a center of civilization surrounded and impinged upon by barbarians (Chang 1982:3). However, not all barbarians were treated equivalently, depending upon their distance, value as allies or subjects, or security threat, among other considerations. "Inner barbarians" mostly occupied the contiguous border regions within the empire, tended to be more similar to the Chinese, were often transplanted from elsewhere, and were placed in military districts; "outer barbarians," such as the Hsiung-nu, were organized into dependent tributary states, often functioning as buffers between the center and other less-pacified barbarians (Eadie 1977:231–232; cf. Lattimore 1962:480; Chang 1982:2–3; Kratochwil 1986:31; Barfield 2001:15–16).

Beginning at least as early as the Shang civilization, Chinese society began to assume the form of a distinctive cultural configuration and therefore gave rise to a specific Chinese identity. This characteristic identity evolved further during the nascent Ch'in and Han dynasties to form what has come to be seen as a traditional Chinese cultural and ethnic identity, and as the empire expanded both northward and southward, those peoples incorporated were also required to assimilate this identity as well. To be Chinese was to be civilized; those who could not or would not assimilate remained barbarians (Hall 1989:62). However, in some border regions, some degree of partial acculturation took place, particularly among the social elite, resulting in a hybrid culture that was neither wholly Chinese nor barbarian (Wu 2013).

Rome

Without question the ancient society most studied in respect to the aspects of spatial structure and organization discussed in previous chapters is Rome. At least three book-length studies of the Roman frontier—Dyson's *The Creation of the Roman Frontier* (1985), Whittaker's *Frontiers of the Roman Empire: A Social and Economic Study* (1994) and Elton's *Frontiers of the Roman Empire* (1996)—have been written, in addition to a series of Roman Frontier Studies Congresses (e.g., Birley 1952, Hanson and Keppie 1980, and Maxfield and Dobson 1991).

Rome began as a small settlement on the Tiber River in central Italy c. 900 BC. After several hundred years of domination by the Etruscans, Rome emerged as an autonomous city-state at the end of the

6th century, throwing off monarchical rule and establishing the Republic, which endured for almost five hundred years. After a period of civil war and internal unrest, culminating in the seizure of power by Julius Caesar, the Empire came into being under his adopted nephew Octavian, later Caesar Augustus. The empire lasted another five hundred years or so, declining, collapsing and splitting into eastern and western empires in the 4th and 5th centuries AD.

In the 5th century BC, Rome entered upon a period of peer polity interaction with other city-states in central Italy. Its favorable location gave it an advantage in competition with them, and this competition led to a series of conflicts, during which time in the early Republic the Romans were able to conquer most of their neighbors and enlarge their territory. As they expanded, in addition to other Italic peoples, the Romans also encountered the powerful Etruscan states to the north and east and well-established Greek colonies to the south. By the end of the 3rd century BC most of the Italian peninsula was under Roman political control; however, there was during this period considerable cultural influence—by means of acculturation—from the Greeks and Etruscans. In some instances this control was direct, a process which was facilitated by the establishment of *colonia*, transplanted communities of land-hungry Romans which maintained political control and military security; in other cases, control was exercised more indirectly by means of alliances.

The center of the Roman core zone was always Rome, whether village, town, city, or metropolis. During the early Republic, the Roman core zone expanded as neighboring local cultures were assimilated and granted citizenship. Eventually the Romans gained control over the entire Italian peninsula, which became and essentially remained the core zone through the remainder of the Republic and the Empire. At the northern end of Italy lay the Alps, which functioned both as a strong natural barrier and a filter of traffic in and out of the peninsula, allowing for trade, but limiting the movement of groups southward. The area between the Po River and the Alps was occupied by tribes which could not or would not be incorporated into the core zone, thus serving as a buffer (and border) between the Romanized peninsula to the south and the more remote and hostile Celtic tribes to the north. This configuration lasted almost one hundred and fifty years to almost the end of the Republic, when Julius Caesar conquered Gaul (Dyson 1985:42–43, 173).

5. Case Studies

As the Romans continued to expand outside of Italy, they increasingly came into contact and conflict with the Carthaginians, who, from their base in northern Africa, were also expanding into the western Mediterranean. Their titanic struggle with the Carthaginians in three Punic wars enabled them to establish further provinces in Spain, Sardinia, Sicily and north Africa. All of these additions to Roman territory, and including southern Gaul as well, lay within the Mediterranean geographic and climatic zone. In addition, as Millett observes, "the limits to Roman expansion were determined broadly by the presence of social systems which were adaptable to the Roman administrative system" (1990:38–39). Central and northern Gaul, on the other hand, belonged to continental Europe, offering different ecological and cultural challenges (Dyson 1985:271; cf. Whittaker 1993:134, 1994:93–94). Moreover, whereas the Romans primarily encountered tribes and chiefdoms of varying levels of development in the west, they had to deal with more urbanized, Hellenized state societies in the east, requiring not only different strategies and administrative policies but also different kinds of boundaries, borders and frontiers (Whittaker 1994:49–51; cf. Hodgson 1989:177–178).

In addition to having reached an ecological and cultural boundary in Gaul, as a result of its expansion,

> the Roman state had now developed socio-political and socioeconomic systems which required the constant inflow of raw materials and manpower to maintain their stability. This need, and the endemic militarism of the state, led inexorably to a process of economic exploitation of peripheral areas, followed by conquest. In this way the army and the traders leapfrogged over each other across barbarian Europe, absorbing the largely Celtic tribes into the Roman system [Cunliffe 1988:10].

Caesar's conquest of Gaul brought Rome to another putative barrier, the Rhine River. Although in his *Commentaries* Caesar characterized the Rhine as a cultural barrier, largely for military reasons, archaeological evidence suggests that tribes on the western and eastern banks were not that different at the time of Caesar's incursion, but that by stopping at the Rhine and treating it as a natural barrier, Caesar created the subsequent reality that he had earlier imagined (Cunliffe 1988:117, 170; cf. Dyson 1985:173; Okun 1989; Wells 1992; Whittaker 1993:136; Elton 1996:46–47, 128; Miller 1996:160). Expansion continued during the Prin-

97

cipate and the early empire, adding provinces in Egypt, the Near East, southeastern Europe and Britain (Figure 5). Reece notes that "…whereas the frontiers of the early empire mark the division between Roman peoples and peoples who did not want to be Roman, the later frontiers often mark the division between those who wished to remain Roman and those who wanted to become Roman" (1979:235; cf. Dyson 1985:4).

The driving force of expansion during the Republic and the early empire was the Roman army led by ambitious members of the aristocracy.

It functioned as the motor of the expansion machinery: (1) in economic terms by its immense needs for its mobilization and maintenance; (2) in demographic terms by the recruitment and replacement of soldiers for the legions, auxilia and other irregular units; (3) in socio-political terms by the sheer presence of this organization in the frontier zone and (4) in infrastructural terms by weaving a transportation network over land and water and consequently favouring the pattern of future hierarchical settlement structure by the location of military camps and supply-sites. In this way the army moulded the whole socio-economic structure of the frontier zone [Bloemers 1991:452; cf. Elton 1996:12].

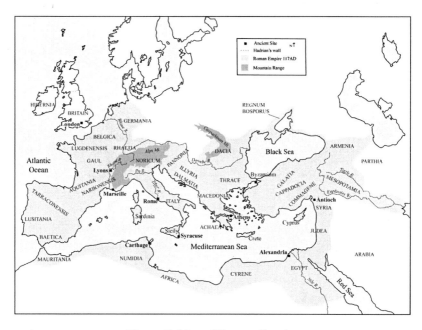

Figure 5: Map of Roman Empire

5. Case Studies

Once new provinces were acquired,

the controlled areas were exploited with a minimum of Roman man-power. During the first century BC and the first half of the first century AD, there were few Romans in the provinces. Those who were present can be divided into three groups: the governor and his administration, the army (which later produced settlers in the form of retired veterans) and merchants. All groups stood out strongly from the native inhabitants and were often unpopular [Elton 1996:15].

As the Romans pushed onward in their continued expansion, a more developed and complex center/periphery structure emerged. The core zone remained the Italian peninsula, which produced the majority of staples such as bread, oil and wine; few areas beyond the core were considered desirable unless they could supply at least one of these staple products (Williams 1998:28; cf. Cunliffe 1988:2). Provinces added outside the core zone, particularly those acquired during the Republic and which, like Gaul and Spain, became highly assimilated, comprised what I would characterize as a border zone, or semi-periphery, intermediate between the core zone and the frontier (cf. Dyson 1985:4). The boundary between border and frontier thus represented "the dividing line between internal and external control" (Whittaker 1994:43).

Cunliffe notes that by the 2nd century AD the core had grown so quickly that it had absorbed much of the periphery without fully integrating it (1988:2; Miller 1996:163). But by the end of the 2nd century AD expansion had slowed and virtually ceased, followed by a period of stagnation before the inevitable contraction began (Woolf 1990:49). Thus,

the Roman Empire on the eve of the barbarian invasions of the late second and third centuries AD had reached the natural limits of its useful economic expansion. Yet the very process of stabilization had created dependent but expanding polities beyond the frontiers which were bound to destroy the conditions for their own existence. The frontier history of the Later Roman Empire then becomes the history of a struggle for finite resources, a competition for the food produced in the frontier zone, while at the same time there was a less efficient use of the resources available [Whittaker 1983:117].

In some areas, such as Gaul and Germany, several levels of decreasing integration can be observed within the border and frontier zones based upon the distribution of imported goods. According to

99

Boundaries, Borders and Frontiers in Archaeology

Hedeager (1987:126), "Two structurally different systems existed on the northern periphery of the Roman Empire at the beginning of the imperial era, one with its roots in the Celtic world, and the other with its roots in the Germanic world." This disparity resulted in three structures or zones: 1) a highly assimilated Romano-Gallic border zone of Romanized Celtic chiefdoms which had already attained a high level of development before their conquest; 2) a buffer zone comprised of less-developed and less-acculturated vassal Celtic kingdoms; 3) Free Germany east of the Rhine, composed of unconquered, independent and unassimilated tribes not under Roman political control, whose development was mediated by contact with the buffer zone.

Within the buffer zone, common and commonly-used items such as pottery and bronze coins have been found in quantity, the result of short-distance trade among the Roman provinces; but beyond the buffer zone were found high-value items of gold, silver, bronze and glass items, primarily vessels involved in eating and drinking, and silver coins acquired through long-distance trade and found almost entirely in the burials of elite warriors and leaders (Hedeager 1979; cf. Groenman-van Waateringe 1980:1042; Bloemers 1983:182–183, 1991:453; Whittaker 1984:74; Fulford 1985:100; Cunliffe 1988:184; Williams 1998:11–12). Such zones of integration reinforce the distinction between borders and frontiers, in that Roman cultural and economic influence extended into the frontier beyond the border area of political and military control.

These differing levels and degrees of incorporation or integration primarily involve the process of acculturation, or more specifically in this instance, Romanization (Slofstra 1983:71). Romanization is one of the most—if not the most—studied and discussed instances of acculturation in the past, with a great deal of consideration given to theoretical and methodological issues including much criticism, modification and revision of earlier constructs (e.g., Millett 1970; Bartel 1980; Slofstra 1983; Reece 1990; Saddington 1991; Clarke 1996; Cooper 1996; Hingely 1996; Gosden 2004:104–105; Pitts 2007; Revell 2009) based upon a vast corpus of empirical data. Just as acculturation has been characterized by some critics as the unilateral imposition of cultural elements on a passive indigenous population, Romanization has been seen, until relatively recently, as a specific example of that process (cf. Millett 1970:2).

5. Case Studies

Typically the first Romans encountered by indigenous groups were traders; they were followed by soldiers, then administrators, and finally, perhaps, settlers or colonists. Roman political control was imposed by force, but Romanization was largely an informal, indirect, and often accidental process initially involving local elites wishing to maintain or enhance their authority and status by associating themselves with and emulating Roman material culture, manners, and ideology (Millett 1990:38; Saddington 1991:413; cf. Eadie 1977:232–233; Haselgrove 1984:15; Higham 1989:154; Hingely 1996:40–41; Williams 1998:27). Thus the diffusion of Roman cultural elements largely occurred as the result of choice and selection on the part of other cultures both within and outside of Roman political or military control (Eadie 1977:232–233; Woolf 1998; cf. Hingely 1996:44). In highly Romanized provinces such as Gaul, acculturation occurred through all levels of Celtic society, with an equivalent mutual Roman acculturation, resulting in a hybrid Gallo-Roman population (Bloemers 1983:162–163; Roymans 1983:56; Woolf 1998; Gosden 2004:106). However, in more distant and more marginal environments lacking a cooperative elite, such as the pre-desert region of Libya, the effect of Romanization was considerably more limited (Grahame 1998; cf. Clarke 1996:83).

Likewise, the range of responses to the diffusion of Roman culture ranged from rejection and resistance, to partial acculturation, to assimilation (Millar et al. 1967:10; Woolf 1998). This diversity of response is evident at every level of organization within the Roman empire, i.e., not only within the empire itself, but within provinces, communities and even families (Haselgrove 1990; Jones 1997:135; Revell 2009:ix; Mattingly 2010:289). Often this resulted in an elite class which was fully assimilated, wishing to be and to be seen as Roman as possible; those who emulated local elites at least to some extent, becoming partially acculturated; and a large lower class which mostly resisted Romanization (Millar et al. 1967:228; Okun 1989:135; Webster 2001).

In most instances, although Romanization was desirable and beneficial to Romans—or mutually beneficial and desirable for both Roman and indigenous elites—the major factor influencing acculturation was self-interest on the part of various elements of the local population (Okun 1989:136). And whereas members of the local elites strove to emulate Roman behavior as closely as possible in order to fit in and be acceptable, members of the lower orders were more likely to adapt or modify elements of Roman culture, resulting in a greater measure of hybridization (Okun 1989:135). Although individual aspects of Roman culture diffused beyond the empire's political and military control, the process of Romanization ceased at the boundary of the *limes*, suggesting that the desire to be Roman—or perhaps to *seem* Roman—was limited to those areas in which *Romanitas* conveyed significant benefit (Woolf 1998:18; cf. Cooper 1996).

One area in which considerable acculturation—or more precisely, syncretism—occurred was in the realm of religion (Millar et al. 1967:11; Bloemers 1983:170; Higham 1984:169; King 1990:236–237). Such blending and modification was facilitated by the polytheistic nature of both Roman and most non-Roman Iron Age systems of belief and practice, which more easily accommodated the addition of deities, rites and beliefs than monotheistic religions. Hence the strong resistance to Romanization by Jews and, subsequently, Christians.

Frontier buffer zones tended to be areas outside of direct Roman military or political control, and therefore interaction between border and buffer zones was primarily economic in nature, although their primary significance for Rome was the military protection they provided by their location between Roman territory and more hostile barbarians (Hanson 1989:56; Bloemers 1991:452–453). Vassal or client states (many of which were in fact tribes or chiefdoms) ruled by "friendly kings" provided not only tribute and trade markets, but also protection where resources could not support a Roman military presence (Braund 1984:91–95, 1989; Whittaker 1984:67). Braund (1984:182) notes that such entities were both inside and outside the empire depending upon how both they and the Romans chose to construe their status, role and position. However,

> the survival of Roman frontier systems, from an economic standpoint, was only marginally dependent on societies outside the frontier. To a large extent the frontiers form the outer limit of a self-contained world. Even for communities in the immediate hinterland within the frontiers, there was a mixed degree of dependence which varied both regionally and chronologically according to local circumstances such as social organisation and farming economy [Fulford 1984:90].

As expansion slowed and eventually ceased, the informal boundaries established during the Republic, which were enforced primarily through bribery and the threat of force, were replaced with more formal

5. Case Studies

and permanent armed fortifications, first along the Rhine and Danube rivers and later in Africa and the Near East (Dyson 1985:275; Williams 1998:8, 24; cf. Millar et al. 1967:104–105; Elton 1996; Hanson 1984:57–58; 1996:126). Provincial boundaries, however, were only occasionally marked by boundary stones or ditches, along with natural boundaries such as mountain ranges or rivers (Elton 1996:127; cf. Hanson 1984:55).

Rivers were the most common demarcation of borders, even though they also functioned as routes of communication and trade and the cultures on either side were often more similar than different (Whittaker 1994:56). Often linear barriers were considered equivalent to rivers as boundaries, and the two forms of boundary were never used together except as complementary parts of a larger boundary system. Linear barriers or fortifications had a primarily military function, but were mostly designed to permit trade and filter trans-boundary movement rather than completely cut off communication (Hanson 1984:58–60; cf. van der Leeuw 1983:17). Earlier boundaries emphasized the differences between Roman civilization and barbarism, but as later boundaries receded and collapsed under barbarian incursions, their significance as dividing lines decreased (Olster 1996:94–101; Miller 1996:161–164; cf. Whittaker 1984:68, 1994:122, 223; Elton 1996:126).

In conclusion, Whittaker offers four propositions concerning Roman frontiers (which in the terminology I employ in this book includes borders as well), particularly those in the west: (1) they normally cut through areas of relative cultural homogeneity rather than separating them; (2) they can be explained with reference to Lattimore's model of economic marginality; (3) there was a symbiotic relationship of exchange between border and frontier which created social and economic integration; (4) frontiers are, by the very nature of their existence, agents of their own destruction (1984:66–69). He also notes several paradoxes in respect to Roman frontiers, i.e., although Rome was "from the beginning ... a society of frontiers" (Dyson 1985:7), there is no evidence of what might be considered a frontier policy until Caesar Augustus; and although Rome was "a society deeply committed from its very earliest laws to the juridical and sacral definition of boundaries, yet it is virtually impossible at any given time either before or after Augustus to discover where the outer limits of those boundaries were drawn" (Whittaker 1994:11).

It is perhaps not surprising that the two great civilizations of China and Rome have been compared and contrasted not only by scholars of both societies, but by comparative frontier historians as well. The most thorough and complete of these are by Lattimore (1962, 1979, 1980) and Eadie (1977). Lattimore notes that both the Chinese and the Romans constructed extensive walled boundaries which, although they were ostensibly created to keep out the barbarians, actually were primarily designed to limit their own expansion because "In all such cases, the establishment of the frontier marks the zone beyond which the further expansion of empire would cost more in military and administrative expenditures than could be paid for by increased revenues" (1979:37–38; cf. 1962:116–117; cf. Eadie 1977:223). He also describes how both societies utilized a "divide and rule" strategy toward barbarians, including engaging some of them as mercenaries (1980:208).

Eadie's analysis focuses upon the structure and function of frontiers in China under the Former Dynasty (202 BC–AD 8) and the early Roman empire (44 BC–AD 284) "because the imperial ambitions of both societies disrupted existing tribal associations in the territories they occupied and precipitated long-term conflicts on their northern borders" (1977:216). He points out, however, that the internal organization and subsistence levels of these barbarian groups were not identical, since the Hsiung-nu were nomadic pastoralists, while the German tribes were largely sedentary and practiced a mixed economy of agriculture and pastoralism. He also observes that while the Chinese began building the Great Wall during the creation of the empire by the Ch'in dynasty, the Romans did not construct such fortifications until the 2nd century AD, and that these fortifications did not play a significant role in the defense of the empire (1977:223).

According to Eadie "A deep-seated and ineradicable belief in their cultural superiority vis-a-vis the barbarians shaped the frontier policies of both societies. For the Romans and Chinese alike genuine equality with untutored barbarians was impossible; only when the northern tribes had surrendered and had been 'educated' in Chinese/Roman ways would they be admitted to imperial society" (1977:231). And both governments evolved administrative structures and procedures for assimilating and "civilizing" barbarians, as well as organizing frontier barbarians into client kingdoms or tributary states (Eadie 1977:231). Whittaker also notes that not only did the expansion of both Rome and China follow Lattimore's model of economic marginality, but both civilizations advanced not to a fixed line of cultivation, but rather into a zone of mixed farming where there was a transition from agriculture to pastoralism (1994:93). We will shortly see that this model applies to Mycenaean civilization as well (cf. Feuer 2015).

Late Bronze Age Thessaly

The third and final case study, Mycenaean Thessaly, differs from those of China and Rome in a number of ways. To begin with, Mycenaean civilization did not achieve either the time span or the territorial extent of Rome or China. Moreover, although the relationship between the state-level societies of Bronze Age Greece can be characterized in terms of peer polity interaction, as was the case in the early history of both China and Rome, a Mycenaean empire did not evolve out of such interaction. Finally, rather than present an overview "big picture" of Mycenaean civilization, as with Rome and China, I have chosen to focus here on one part of the Mycenaean periphery, the province of Thessaly and specifically aspects of acculturation discussed earlier in Chapter 5, and which has been the focus of much of my most recent research (e.g., Feuer 2011, 2015, 2016).

The core area of Mycenaean civilization was located in central and southern Greece (Figure 6). It was in this core zone that Mycenaean civilization first emerged and evolved, reaching a level of economic, political and social development equivalent to contemporary societies in the Near East, Egypt and Anatolia (Feuer 1994, 1999, 2004; Shelton 2010). Many aspects of Mycenaean civilization originated in the indigenous mainland Middle Helladic culture (Dickinson 1972, 1977; cf. Dietz 1988; Galaty and Parkinson 2007; Voutsaki 2010) in a more or less continuous development, such as the evolution of shaft graves from earlier cist graves and of early Mycenaean pottery from Middle Helladic forms. There was, however, also a rapid expansion of power and wealth in the early Mycenaean or Shaft Grave period (Late Helladic I-II, c. 1600–1400 BC) which led to a transformation of the relatively small and poor Middle Helladic chiefdoms into the wealthy and powerful states of Late Helladic III (c. 1400–1200 BC), and part of the impetus for these developments came from contact with and influence from Crete and the Cycladic Islands (Dickinson 1972, 1984; Hägg 1982; Laffineur 1989;

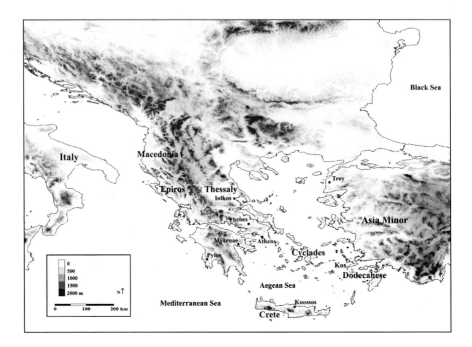

Figure 6: Map of Bronze Age Aegean

Rutter 1993; Voutsaki 2001; Galaty and Parkinson 2007; Wright 2008). This influence can be seen particularly in the development of a palatial society with a complex political, social and economic organization and in the creation of distinctive art and pottery. It was a synthesis of these traditions and influences which led to a society which was neither Middle Helladic, Minoan nor Cycladic, but a fusion of these elements, which came to be known as Mycenaean civilization.

As the emerging Mycenaean elites looked outward for trade opportunities to enhance their wealth, status, and power, they became increasingly involved in the extensive eastern Mediterranean exchange network, establishing relationships throughout the Aegean with other local elites; it seems that for the most part they were seeking metals and rare or exotic raw materials, in return for which they traded finished craft products. Other variables influencing the nature and degree of Mycenaeanization were geography and the kinds of societies within the Mycenaean orbit. The geography determined what resources might be attractive to Mycenaean traders as well as the needs and desires of

5. Case Studies

the local inhabitants, particularly local elites who were controlling access to those resources (Feuer 2015, 2016). These trading relationships of course involved social and political aspects as well. It is possible, however, that even if an elite class within a given society became Mycenaeanized, other elements or groups within that society might have resisted or rejected Mycenaeanization or adopted only certain aspects of Mycenaean culture, resulting in a spectrum of acculturation.

Initial contact may have been initiated by adventurous individuals or groups in search of opportunities, first sporadically or intermittently, and subsequently increasing in tempo and frequency; very likely these encounters would have involved *inter alia* ceremonial gift exchange and feasting (cf., e.g., Dietler 1989, 1997, 1998, 2005). These preliminary phases would have established relationships and patterns of interaction leading to more intensive and institutionalized social and economic networks. Archaeological evidence indicates that material items, most prominently pottery, were the first elements of Mycenaean culture to be accepted, followed by methods and techniques, and finally social, political and religious ideology.

In the most heavily Mycenaeanized areas all of these aspects of Mycenaean culture were borrowed and adapted; in the least Mycenaeanized locales, borrowing may have been primarily restricted to pottery and some other aspects of material culture. Initially items would have been obtained through exchange, but eventually in many areas, accompanying technology transfer, products would have been made by itinerant or resident Mycenaean craftspeople and/or local craftworkers. It has generally been assumed that the more borrowed aspects of culture are present, the greater the degree of acculturation. Moreover, certain cultural elements or kinds of artifacts have been considered to be possible Mycenaean ethnic or cultural markers or diacritics, integral rather than marginal elements of Mycenaean culture or identity. For Mycenaean civilization, some of the most distinctive cultural markers included tholos and chamber tombs, the megaron, bronze weapons, the Linear B script, figurines, pottery, sealstones and certain kinds of jewelry (Feuer 2004; 2011, 512–513).

Thessaly, in north-central Greece, is one of its largest and most geographically varied provinces, and as a result can be subdivided into a number of constituent subregions (Figure 7). The southeastern

107

coastal region should be considered part of the northern Aegean area, with a Mediterranean climate allowing for the cultivation of vines and olives, and like other coastal Aegean locales is easily accessible by sea, facilitating trade and communication.

The inland plains to the north and west, however, are part of a transitional ecological zone more similar to the climate, topography and vegetation of the European continent rather than to the Mediterranean coastal environment and the Mycenaean core area further south. This environment was less hospitable to the Mycenaean subsistence economy—which in addition to fish, wheat and barley relied heavily on vines and olives—and lacked other resources attractive to

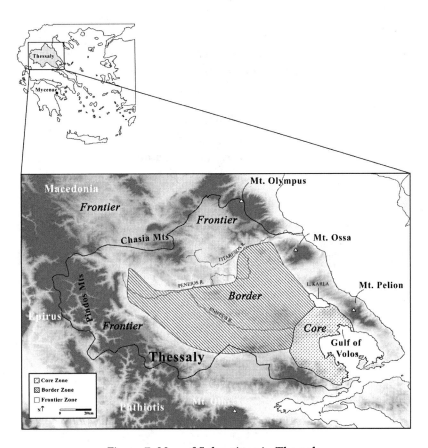

Figure 7: Map of Subregions in Thessaly

108

5. Case Studies

the Mycenaean states of the core zone, which seems to have been oriented more toward maritime trade and communication than exploitation of the inland plains (Feuer 1983:188–190; 1994; 2003; 2014). These large interior areas can be further subdivided into eastern and western plains divided by a line of foothills running in a northwest-southeast direction.

The third topographical region within Thessaly is comprised of the impressive Pindos and Chasia mountains to the west and north respectively. Although this environment is suitable for grazing, agriculture is difficult except in small, isolated valleys, temperatures are more extreme, and rainfall is more abundant. In other words, this part of Thessaly is inhospitable to sedentary habitation and represents a formidable barrier to movement, transportation and communication except by way of a few narrow passes (Feuer 1983:32–38, 91–92).

Beginning in the seventh millennium BC Thessaly was one of the earliest regions of Greece to be settled by sedentary agriculturalists, who established a prosperous tribal society living in villages. For most of the ensuing millennia (c. 7000–3000 BC) Thessaly therefore comprised the core zone of Neolithic Greece. Although the number of settlements increased and villages became larger over time there was little distinction among different parts of the area, with the exception of several more developed sites near the coast. In the succeeding Early Bronze Age (c. 3000–2000 BC) the coastal zone appears to have evolved more rapidly than the interior plains, but the distinctions between the two subregions were still not significant. During the Middle Bronze Age (c. 2000–1600 BC), however, an era which has not yet been thoroughly investigated in Thessaly, it appears that the coastal region followed the developmental trends further south in the core zone, while the inland plains continued at the same level as previously (Dickinson 1977; Feuer 1983:48–49, 2004).

This divergence continued and increased during the Late Helladic I-II periods, the beginning of the Late Bronze Age (c. 1600–1400 BC), and the formative period of Mycenaean civilization. Developments in southeastern Thessaly largely mirrored those further south, while areas further inland continued in the same fashion as heretofore. In LH III (c. 1400–1200 BC), Mycenaean civilization in the core zone reached its peak of development, reflected in the establishment of proto-state societies with highly developed social and economic institutions. These

109

same processes occurred in the coastal zone, although the polity which existed there does not appear to have achieved the level of power and complexity of the palaces of Mycenae and Pylos (Feuer 1983:49–53, 1994, 1999, 2003, 2004; Pantou 2010).

In addition to these developments within the core zone, Mycenaean civilization expanded beyond the core zone to areas in the Mediterranean basin, including Crete, the Cyclades, the Dodecanese, western Anatolia, and Italy. Another area of expansion was the inland plains of Thessaly. Some elements of Mycenaean culture are present there, but not the full range of the assemblage found in the core zone. Moreover, elements of the local indigenous culture persist, so that in burials (about which we have more archaeological knowledge than settlements) there is a mixture of cultural elements, which is what, given my previous discussion of border zones, one would expect. Whereas there is evidence of centralized and institutionalized political, social and economic structures in the coastal zone, these functions seem to be more decentralized further inland (Feuer 1983:204–206, 1999, 2003, 2004; Feuer and Schneider 2003).

Thus during LH III Thessaly appears to have been comprised of three zones of decreasing integration: the coastal zone, which is similar to, but perhaps not as highly developed as the Mycenaean core area further south; the interior plains, a border zone wherein the indigenous population had become partially acculturated, with an overlay of Mycenaean culture; and the frontier zone comprised of the foothills and mountains to the north and west of the interior plains, which was barely penetrated by Mycenaean civilization (Feuer 1983:204–206, 1994, 1999; cf. Andreou et al. 1996:559). I would thus assert that cultural variation in Thessaly can be roughly correlated with equivalent geographical and climatic variation and that these three subregions can be characterized as core, border and frontier zones (Figure 7) respectively (Feuer 1983:179–200), or from a world systems perspective, core, semi-periphery and periphery (Wallerstein 1974). I further assert that the degree and nature of acculturation—i.e., Mycenaeanization—similarly varied in each of these subregions (cf. Andreou et al. 1996:550), and in the ensuing discussion I will elaborate these distinctions, beginning with the coastal region, then the interior plains, and finally the surrounding mountains (Figure 8).

The coastal region, as noted above, is that part of Thessaly most

5. Case Studies

similar to the Mycenaean core zone of southern and central Greece in climate, topography, and maritime orientation. Perhaps not surprisingly, then, it also shares considerable cultural similarities as well, so much so that it can in fact be considered the northernmost extension of the core Mycenaean area. This connection, which can be most clearly seen at the site of Pevkakia in the Gulf of Volos, can be traced back at least as far as the Middle Bronze Age, when it shared most, if not all of the characteristic features of Middle Helladic society (Maran 1992; cf. Voutsaki 2010:100). There appears to have been some delay in the adoption of these features compared to their origination and development in the Peloponnese and elsewhere—a phenomenon echoed in the later process of Mycenaean ethnogenesis (Dickinson 1977)—but this may be attributed at least in part to the region's relative remoteness from the sources of change.

Likewise, as Middle Helladic society slowly evolved in MH III and LH I, due in part to Minoan and Cycladic influence, a similar evolution occurred, albeit even more slowly, in coastal Thessaly as well. A significant difference, however, was that this external influence, i.e., Minoanization, was almost entirely indirect at this considerable

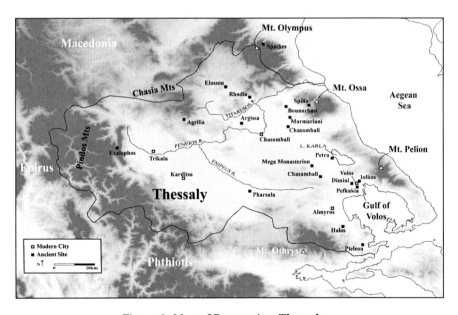

Figure 8: Map of Bronze Age Thessaly

111

remove from its Cretan source and Cycladic intermediaries, and thus Minoanization in southeastern Thessaly ranged from extremely minimal to non-existent (Dickinson 1977:100; Mountjoy 1999:823). On the other hand, by the end of LH II, this area appears to have been fully within the Mycenaean orbit. The initial phases of this process are difficult to discern, just as they are further south aside from Mycenae itself and parts of Messenia, but this is largely because Mycenaean ethnogenesis was a sporadic process identifiable initially only by minimal criteria such as LH I pottery and shaft graves, both of which were uncommon and highly localized even within the Peloponnese (Dickinson 1977; Adrimi-Sismani 2007; cf. Maran 1995:67).

By LH IIB or LH IIIA1 at the latest, however, the coastal zone is virtually indistinguishable from other regions of the Mycenaean core zone. Almost all of the defining characteristics of Mycenaean civilization are present, most notably at the centers of Dimini and Iolkos. These include large public structures, tholos tombs, chamber tombs, a wide range of decorated, plain and monochrome pottery, figurines, Linear B, sealstones and jewelry and other decorative items in a variety of rare and imported materials including gold, amber, faience, glass paste, and semiprecious stones. The excavator of Dimini contends that it was a palatial center equivalent to those further south (Adrimi-Sismani 2007:167), and although this claim has been disputed and/or modified (e.g., Pantou 2010) it seems clear that there was an elite class comprised of several families which controlled valuable resources and labor, engaged in production and trade, and constructed large buildings and tholos tombs. If it is accepted that this subregion was part of the core area of Mycenaean civilization, then by definition it was completely Mycenaeanized, at least as completely as most of southern and central Greece. The existence of a group of small tholoi and chamber tombs in the vicinity of Almyros may indicate other less powerful elites in this area as well (Adrimi-Sismani 2007:174).

The inland plains, on the other hand, were largely cut off from communication with the coastal zone, and by extension, with the Mycenaean core zone in central and southern Greece, with only a few narrow passes enabling movement, trade, and transportation. There was an opening between the foothills of Mt. Pelion and Mt. Othrys, but only the area immediately north of it was as Mycenaeanized as early and almost as completely as the coastal zone (Figure 8). The sites of Petra and Velestino (ancient Pherae) were large, populous and seemingly prosperous, and the nearby chamber tombs at Mega Monastiri were rich, suggesting at least one, if not more, elite family which controlled the valuable agricultural and lacustrine resources of the plain and of Lake Karla (Adrimi-Sismani 2007:172–173). This area may be considered an extension of the core zone, or, more plausibly, an intermediate border area transitional between the coast and the broad interior plains.

The remainder of the eastern plain is also transitional, both geographically and culturally. The climate is more continental, with heavier rainfall and greater extremes in temperature, well suited for growing cereals and livestock, but not for olives or vines. It was densely populated during the Neolithic, and although the Bronze Age is less well investigated due to the lack of excavated settlements, it appears that the Bronze Age population was descended from Neolithic forebears and may have represented a different ethnicity than that of the coastal region. The material culture of this area seems to have been more conservative than the coastal region, at least partly due to its relative isolation (Feuer 1983:91–92). The most extensively excavated Bronze Age site in this part of Thessaly, Argissa, was a large settlement which existed throughout the Middle Bronze Age, but unlike Pevkakia, demonstrates little evidence of contact with the outside world other than a limited amount of Minyan and Matt-Painted pottery and some influence from the adjoining region of Macedonia (Milojčić 1955; Maran 1992; Horejs 2007).

In the Late Bronze Age, elements of Mycenaean culture are discernible no earlier than LH III and, based on limited settlement evidence, were accepted differentially. It is difficult to assess the nature of sociopolitical organization in the plains, but clearly it was not as advanced or complex as in the coastal region, which itself, as noted, may not have achieved the level of state centralization as elsewhere in Greece. A tribal or chiefdom level of organization seems likely, possibly the latter since there is some evidence for the existence of local elites in some locales. During the Late Bronze Age, there were some impressively large sites such as Bounarbasi, Marmariani and Rhodia (Figure 8) with an abundance of Mycenaean pottery on the surface, as well as a number of small tholos tombs which might have contained the remains of local chiefs and their families (Feuer 1983:188–189). These

113

tombs, and a few others, suggest that a small number of inhabitants of the interior plains became quite Mycenaeanized. One might also include several groups of chamber tombs on and around Mt. Ossa, although in the modern political configuration they belong to the province of Macedonia (Poulaki-Pantermali 1991). However, there is less evidence that the great proportion of the population adopted many elements of Mycenaean material culture—let alone social, political or ideological aspects thereof—other than certain kinds of pottery.

This situation is similar in the western plain as well, though with the exception of the Enipeus River drainage and the vicinity of Pharsala (Adrimi-Sismani 2007:175), it appears not to have been as densely settled. In fact, the northern half of the western plain, which may have been flooded during much of the time in question, occupied by hostile nomadic pastoralists—and possibly therefore yet another ethnic population or cultural group—or otherwise unsuitable for agriculture, seems to have been largely unoccupied during the Late Bronze Age (Feuer 1983:125–126). The presence of a large tholos tomb at Georgikon and several chamber tombs in the vicinity of Pharsala may also indicate a small number of highly Mycenaeanized families, but otherwise the evidence for Mycenaeanization in the western plain is mostly limited to pottery.

Finally, there is the third ecological zone comprising part of modern Thessaly, although it was clearly outside the Mycenaean realm in the Late Bronze Age, since there are no areas within it that are suitable for sedentary agriculture. Today it is mostly inhabited by nomadic pastoralists (Chang and Tourtellotte 1993) belonging to several cultures and ethnicities, and it is not unlikely that this was also the case in the Bronze Age (cf., e.g., Wilkie 1999). These peoples were even less Mycenaeanized than those of the plains; the only evidence for elements of Mycenaean material culture comes from some groups of cist graves at sites such as Agrilia, although there are some similar cist grave burials at the edge of the plain at Chasambali and Exalophos (Feuer 1983:129–141; Eder 2009). Like similar cist graves in Epiros, the primary evidence of, and interest in, Mycenaean culture and technology is the presence of bronze weapons, although some Mycenaean pottery (some handmade) accompanies them, along with somewhat crude handmade local wares (cf. Kilian 1990:448).

In addition to the possible influence of distance on integration

5. Case Studies

into the Mycenaean sociopolitical system, environmental variation seems to account in part for the differences described above. While the coastal zone closely resembles the climate and vegetation of the core zone further south, the inner plains represent a transition between the Mediterranean climate of the south and the continental climate of Europe, with greater extremes of temperature and greater rainfall, which does not allow the cultivation of olives and grapes. Moving further northward and westward into the surrounding mountains, one encounters an environment unsuitable for agriculture but adaptable to nomadic pastoralism (Feuer 1983, 1994, 1999, 2014).

Having presented and examined evidence for the adoption of Mycenaean culture in Thessaly, I will conclude by discussing the phenomenon of Mycenaeanization as a manifestation of culture change and acculturation at the periphery of the Mycenaean world. Beginning with the core zone—the southeastern coastal region of Thessaly—it seems quite clear that this area, with its proximity to southern and central Greece, with a similar climate and topography and an earlier affinity for the social, political, economic and cultural developments which occurred there, belongs within that core zone. The existence of a complex of administrative centers and a level of social, political and economic organization similar if not equivalent to the early state societies of southern and central Greece indicates a similar structure involving an elite class which controlled agricultural and craft production and engaged in the exchange of objects and ideas with other polities (but cf. Andreou et al. 1996:550–551, 559; Pantou 2010). The process of ethnogenesis in other parts of the core zone which led to the development of what we have come to term Mycenaean civilization occurred here as well, though perhaps not as early or as fully as in the Argolid or Messenia. The presence of "palatial" structures, elaborate and richly furnished tombs, a complete repertoire of ceramic vessels (including figurines) produced since at least LH IIIA1 by kilns at Dimini and Pherai, as well as the use of Linear B and sealstones, all testify not only to the complete Mycenaeanization of this region, but its position as the northernmost extension of the Mycenaean core zone (cf. Eder 2009).

In the border zone, however, the eastern and western interior plains, the available evidence suggests that Mycenaeanization occurred later and was more variable. While the areas in the vicinity of Lake

115

Karla and Pharsala, primarily due to their proximity to the core zone, appear to have adopted many aspects of Mycenaean culture, these developments are not apparent, for the most part, until LH III. The presence of small tholoi and chamber tombs in this region suggests that some degree of social differentiation had taken place and that a number of local elite families had become fully Mycenaeanized. However, elsewhere in the plains further north the picture is more uncertain. This uncertainty derives at least in part from the lack of well-excavated settlements from the Late Bronze Age and thus a greater reliance upon data from burials and surface finds in order to evaluate the extent of acculturation.

The most visible evidence of Mycenaeanization is the existence of LH III pottery throughout the region, but the relative scarcity of unpainted ware—unlike, e.g., at Dimini, where unpainted pottery comprised c. 75 percent of the total assemblage (Adrimi-Sismani 1999)—and the limited repertoire of vessel types suggest that the local population, as elsewhere in the Mycenaean periphery, may have accepted and borrowed the set of eating and drinking equipment used in ceremonial feasting or for social occasions while retaining their traditional local pottery and other artifacts for their daily activities. Moreover, it is very likely that the great majority of this pottery was produced by one or more local workshops, i.e., within the plains themselves, rather than imported from the coastal zone. Unlike the upwardly striving elite class, this Late Bronze Age equivalent of peasant farmers may have seen no compelling need to acquire any other elements of Mycenaean civilization.

It is possible, therefore, that this large indigenous agricultural population retained a distinctive local identity; indeed, given the relative scarcity of settlement in the northwestern plain, which could have been occupied by tribes of pastoralists or even foragers, there may have been several ethnic or cultural groups in Thessaly at this time. This premise might be further supported if in fact, as I have suggested elsewhere, that Mycenaean ethnic identity may have been restricted primarily or entirely to the elite class. If this were so, the local elites in the border zone might have been highly Mycenaeanized, but might not necessarily have considered themselves or been considered Mycenaean (Feuer 2011:528–530).

In the mountainous frontier region to the north—and to the west

5. Case Studies

if one includes the Pindos Mountains which are in the modern province of Epiros—both the climate and topography limit occupation essentially to nomadic pastoralists and therefore the primary archaeological evidence is in the form of cist grave cemeteries. The most striking features of these burials are mixed assemblages containing imitations of Mycenaean pottery, handmade local wares, bronze weapons and jewelry. The degree of Mycenaeanization is thus minimal, restricted to desired bronze artifacts and a limited set of pottery types. Very likely contact between the border and frontier zones was sporadic and confined to minimal exchange and/or hostile encounters.

I have tried here to place the process of Mycenaeanization within a broader context of spatial and geographical variation and have sought to demonstrate that decreasing environmental familiarity and suitability in respect to the core zone of southern and central Greece combined with increasing distance from the core zone resulted in decreasing integration within the Mycenaean cultural system. Thus I have shown that the greatest integration and acculturation occurred in the southeastern coastal zone of Thessaly; that a lesser degree of integration and acculturation took place in the border zone of the interior plains; and that minimal integration and acculturation existed in the mountainous frontier zone at the utmost periphery of the Mycenaean world.

Several factors may be invoked in attempting to understand the differential acculturation which occurred in Late Bronze Age Thessaly, including distance, terrain, ethnicity, and class. The role of distance is fairly straightforward: the more remote the location from the source, the greater the effect of friction in terms of communication and interaction; transportation costs, difficulty of movement, and natural and human barriers can all interfere with the potential free and uninhibited exchange of goods, practices and ideas. Thus the coastal zone was closest and most accessible to the Mycenaean core zone, the interior plains had some contact with the coastal zone, and the frontier zone was more remote and inaccessible.

Not only does the nature of the terrain either facilitate or limit movement and communication, but differences in terrain can also influence the desire or motivation for territorial expansion, migration or acculturation. Similar environments tend to foster similar adaptations, though this is not invariably so. The Mediterranean environment of the southeastern coastal region of Thessaly is most similar to that

117

of central and southern Greece, and its inhabitants evolved a similar economy as well as many other aspects of Mycenaean civilization. The interior zone is transitional between the Mediterranean and Continental climatic and geographic regimes, and might therefore be expected to be receptive to some foreign objects, ideas and practices (in roughly that order) and resistant to others. The mountainous frontier zone, on the other hand, was not only difficult to access, and much different than the Mediterranean zone in which Mycenaean civilization arose and flourished, but also fostered societies generally more resistant to change.

Ethnicity and ethnic identity are often powerful determinants of behavior in the modern world, and although we cannot always accurately assess their importance and impact in earlier societies, it is not unreasonable to assume that adherence or commitment to a specific ethnic identity might influence the tendency or desire to identify—or not to identify—with a different ethnic group (see, e.g., Feuer 2011:507–509). It is often difficult to identify and/or characterize ethnic identity in an archaeological context, but the limited evidence from the border and frontier zones suggests that several ethnic and/or cultural groups occupied different parts of Thessaly, and that, unlike the inhabitants of the coastal zone, they may have been more reluctant to adopt new items, ideas or practices in part because of their primarily non-Mycenaean ethnic affiliations.

Class membership proves to be among the most significant factors in both acceptance of foreign ideas and objects and in their diffusion. Those who belong or aspire to belong to an elite class are in many instances more open to incorporating things from other societies, particularly if they are rare or exotic or if they are seen to enhance or maintain their status vis-a-vis elites in their own or other societies (Dietler 2005; Wells 1980, 1992). There is some reason to believe, therefore, that local or indigenous elites and those who aspired to their status were more highly motivated to adopt aspects of Mycenaean culture which may have been perceived as contributing to their prestige or status.

Taking these factors into consideration, we can now summarize the differential interaction and acculturation which occurred in Thessaly during the Late Bronze Age (cf. Feuer 2003:Figure 5). The coastal zone was closest to—and indeed part of—the Mycenaean core zone, sharing a similar environment and presumably roughly the same cultural and ethnic makeup. Thus developments, no doubt initiated by incipient and/or emergent elites—most notably at the sites of Iolkos, Dimini and Pevkakia, but likely elsewhere (such as the plain of Almyros) as well—but also widely shared by most of the population—followed those further south, i.e., complete assimilation and ultimately ethnogenesis.

The border zone was further from both the coastal zone and the rest of the Mycenaean core zone further south and was also separated from it by hills and mountains which limited entrance to and egress from the interior plains. Moreover, the limited available archaeological evidence suggests that its inhabitants may have been of a different ethnicity or ethnicities descended from indigenous occupants more resistant to change than the coastal population. They became only partially acculturated, adopting a limited repertoire of ceramic artifacts, mostly those associated with ceremonial feasting, and possibly the ceramic technology required to produce them. There was, however, a small element of this population, perhaps several local elite families, most of whom resided in those parts of the interior contiguous to the coastal region, which became almost fully acculturated, adopting not only many elements of Mycenaean material culture, but their burial practices as well.

Finally, the most distant and most inaccessible region is that part of the frontier zone which lies in Thessaly. Almost certainly those who occupied this area were of a different ethnicity than the Mycenaeans, and probably those in the border zone as well. Class may have influenced the minimal and very selective acculturation that occurred here as well, since only an individual with some degree of wealth, power or prestige could have had the desire and the wherewithal to acquire prized Mycenaean weapons.

Some discussion should also be made of the mechanisms by which acculturation took place, i.e., the means of diffusion whereby aspects of Mycenaean culture became accessible to the inhabitants of Thessaly. Although evidence of migration in the archaeological record is often difficult to prove or disprove, there is no indication that any substantial movement of people took place during most of the Late Bronze Age in Thessaly. Thus I infer that the inhabitants of Thessaly became aware of Mycenaean culture as the result of stimulus diffusion, i.e., the transmission of ideas, practices and objects rather than the wholesale movement of groups, although it is possible that a small number of Mycenaeans may have settled there as well.

The most likely means of transmission was undoubtedly trade or exchange carried out by existent or would-be elites. Given its location, the coastal zone was clearly a nexus for such activities, particularly at the sites of Pevkakia and Iolkos, and it seems as if the routes leading into the interior reached at least as far as the sites of Pherae in the east and Pharsala in the west as well. Beyond these areas, it appears that trade and communication were more limited and sporadic. And although nomadic and/or transhumant pastoralists in the frontier zone and possibly the northwestern plain as well may have encountered more sedentary peoples as or if they descended into the plains, evidence—other than the few artifacts discussed above—for such contact is even more limited.

Although clearly some exchange must have occurred for imported Mycenaean artifacts to be found in Thessaly—whether initially as gift exchange or as commercial trade—the majority of artifacts found in the coastal zone and the majority of pottery in the border zone seem to have been locally produced. There is also an imbalance in the archaeological record, since although Mycenaean objects are found in Thessaly beginning in LH II, it is not entirely clear what was exchanged for them, since few if any objects from the border or frontier zone can be identified in the coastal zone or elsewhere. The most plausible inference is that raw materials or perishable goods such as agricultural products were offered in exchange.

In this study I have attempted to survey, describe and discuss aspects of past human spatial structure and organization. I have focused on the key concepts of boundaries, borders and frontiers with the intention not only of defining and understanding them separately—particularly in respect to distinctions between linear boundaries and border and frontier zones—but also the relationships among them. I have also examined in some detail the dominant center/periphery model as a means of envisioning and analyzing spatial relationships, emphasizing not so much the role, power and influence of the center, but rather the significance of the periphery, both as an autonomous entity and in its relationship with the center. Although one of the dominant versions of the core/periphery construct, the world systems model, has some limitations when applied to past societies, it also offers some useful basic ideas, such as an emphasis on human societies as systems of interrelated parts.

I also considered in some detail the kinds of political, economic, social and cultural processes occurring in peripheries, emphasizing in particular how peripheral zones, partly because of their relative lack of restrictions combined with their greater propensity for enabling groups and individuals to encounter the Other, were areas conducive to interaction and change. Such change would include increasing political, economic and social complexity and sociocultural developments including acculturation, hybridization and ethnogenesis.

I also discussed how the perception and organization of space evolved as human society become more complex, from the flexible and diffuse boundaries and peripheries of foragers through the more elaborate center/periphery structure and carefully delineated and defended boundaries of the state and empire. By using examples from contemporary, historical and ethnohistorical contexts as well as those in the archaeological record, I tried to demonstrate the continuity of human behavior in regard to spatial organization. My discussion of boundaries, borders and frontiers concluded by considering in some detail three ancient societies—Chinese, Roman and Mycenaean—which exemplified many of the ideas, perceptions and behaviors relating to human spatial organization.

Bibliography

Abruzzi, William S. 1982. "Ecological Theory and Ethnic Differentiation among Human Populations," *Current Anthropology* 23:13–33.

Adams, William Y. 1981. "Dispersed Minorities of the Middle East: A Comparison and a Lesson," in *Persistent Peoples: Cultural Enclaves in Perspective*, ed. George Pierre Castile, Gilbert Kushner and William Y. Adams, pp. 3–25. Tucson: University of Arizona Press.

Adelman, Jeremy and Stephen Aron. 1999. "From Borderlands to Borders: Empires, Nation-States and the Peoples in between in North American History," *The American Historical Review* 104:814–841.

Adrimi-Sismani, Vasiliki. 1999. "Mykenaïkos Keramikos Klivanos sto Dimini," in *I Peripheria tou Mykenaïkou Kosmou. Praktika A Diethnous Epistemonikou Symposiou, Lamia 25–29 Septemvriou 1994*, ed. Eleni Froussou, pp.131–142. Lamia: Ekdosi ID' Eforias Proistorikon kai Klassikon Archaiotiton.

_____. 2007. "Mycenaean Northern Borders Revisited: New Evidence from Thessaly," in *Rethinking Mycenaean Palaces II*, 2nd rev. ed., ed. Michael L. Galaty and William A. Parkinson, pp. 159–177. Cotsen Institute of Archaeology Monograph 60. Los Angeles: Cotsen Institute of Archaeology.

Alden, John R. 1979. "A Reconstruction of Toltec Period Political Units in the Valley of Mexico," in *Transformations: Mathematical Approaches to Culture Change*, ed. Colin Renfrew and Kenneth L. Cooke, pp. 169–200. New York: Academic Press.

Alexander, John. 1977. "The 'Frontier' Concept in Prehistory: the End of the Moving Frontier," in *Hunters, Gatherers and First Farmers Beyond Europe*, ed. J. V. S. Megaw, pp. 25–40. Leicester: Leicester University Press.

_____, and Abbas Mohammed. 1982. "Frontier Theory and the Neolithic Period in Nubia," in *Nubian Studies: Proceedings of the Symposium for Nubian Studies, Selwyn College, Cambridge, 1978*, ed. J.M. Plumley, pp. 34–40. Warminster: Aris & Phillips Ltd.

Alexander, Rani T. 1998. "Afterword: Toward an Archaeological Theory of Culture Contact," in *Studies in Culture Contact: Interaction, Culture Change, and Archaeology*, ed. James G. Cusick, pp. 476–495. Center for Archaeological Investigations, Occasional Paper No. 25. Carbondale: Southern Illinois University.

Alvarez, Robert R. Jr. 1995. "The Mexican-US Border: The Making of an Anthropology of Borderlands," *Annual Review of Anthropology* 24:447–470.

123

Bibliography

Amory, Patrick. 1997. *People and Identity in Ostrogothic Italy, 489–554.* Cambridge: Cambridge University Press.

Anderson, James, and Liam O'Dowd. 1999. "Borders, Border Regions and Territoriality: Contradictory Meanings, Changing Significance," *Regional Studies* 33:593–604.

Anderton, Douglas L. 1986. "Intermarriage of Frontier Immigrant, Religious and Residential Groups: An Examination of Macrostructural Assimilation," *Sociological Inquiry* 56:341–353.

Andreou, Stelios. 2001. "Exploring the Patterns of Power in the Bronze Age Settlements of Northern Greece," in *Urbanism in the Aegean Bronze Age,* ed. Keith Branigan, pp. 160–173. Sheffield Studies in Aegean Archaeology 4. London: Sheffield Academic Press.

_____, Michael Fotiadis and Kostas Kotsakis. 1996. "Review of Aegean Prehistory V: The Neolithic and Bronze Age of Northern Greece," *American Journal of Archaeology* 100:537–597.

Antonaccio, Carla. 2003. "Hybridity and the Cultures within Greek Culture," in *The Cultures within Ancient Greek Culture: Contact, Conflict, Collaboration,* ed. Carol Dougherty and Leslie Kurke, pp. 57–74. Cambridge: Cambridge University Press.

Arafat, Karim, and Catherine Morgan. 1994. "Athens, Etruria and the Heuneburg: Mutual Misconceptions in the Study of Greek-Barbarian Relations," in *Classical Greece: Ancient Histories and Modern Archaeologies,* ed. Ian Morris, pp. 108–134. Cambridge: Cambridge University Press.

Armillas, Pedro. 1987. "Unity and Diversity in the Ancient Mesoamerican Civilization," in *The Boundaries of Civilizations in Space and Time,* ed. Matthew Melko and Leighton R. Scott, pp. 64–66. Lanham, MD: University Press of America.

Asiwaju, Anthony Ijaola. 1986. "Problem Solving Along African Borders: The Nigeria-Benin Case," in *Across Boundaries: Transborder Interaction in Comparative Perspective,* ed. Oscar J. Martinez, pp. 159–187. El Paso: Texas Western Press.

Axelrod, Robert. 1997. "The Dissemination of Culture: A Model with Local Convergence and Global Polarization," *The Journal of Conflict Resolution* 41:203–226.

Axtell, James. 1981. "The English Colonial Impact on Indian Culture," in *The European and the Indian: Essays in the Ethnohistory of Colonial North America,* pp. 245–271. Oxford: Oxford University Press.

Banks, Marcus. 1966. *Ethnicity: Anthropological Constructions.* London: Routledge.

Bannon, John Francis. 1970. *The Spanish Borderlands Frontier, 1513–1821.* New York: Holt, Rinehart and Winston.

Barfield, Thomas J. 1989. *The Perilous Frontier: Nomadic Empires and China.* Oxford: Basil Blackwell.

_____. 2001. "The Shadow Empires: Imperial State Formation Along the Chinese-Nomad Frontier," in *Empires: Perspectives from Archaeology and History,* ed. Susan E. Alcock, Terence N. D'Altroy, Kathleen D. Morrison and Carla M. Sinopoli, pp. 10–41. Cambridge: Cambridge University Press.

Bartel, Brad. 1980. "Colonialism and Cultural Responses: Problems Related to Roman Provincial Analysis," *World Archaeology* 12:11–26.

Bibliography

Barth, Fredrik. 1969. "Introduction," in *Ethnic Groups and Boundaries: The Social Organization of Cultural Difference*, ed. Fredrik Barth, pp. 9–38. Boston: Little, Brown and Company.

_____. 2000. "Boundaries and Connections," in *Signifying Identities: Anthropological Perspectives on Boundaries and Contested Values*, ed. Anthony P. Cohen, pp. 17–36. London: Routledge.

Berkhofer, Robert F., Jr. 1981. "The North American Frontier as Process and Context," in *The Frontier in History: North America and Southern Africa Compared*, ed. Howard Lamar and Leonard Thompson, pp. 43–75. New Haven: Yale University Press.

Bhabha, Homi K. 1996. "Cultures In-Between," in *Questions of Cultural Identity*, ed. Stuart Hall and Paul du Gay, pp. 53–60. London: Sage Publications.

_____. 2004. *The Location of Culture*. London: Routledge.

Bilde, Per, Troels Engberg-Pedersen, Lise Hannestad, Jan Zahle and Klavs Randsborg. 1993. "Preface," in *Centre and Periphery in the Hellenistic World*, ed. Per Bilde, Troels Engberg-Pedersen, Lise Hannestad, Jan Zahle and Klavs Randsborg, pp. 9–13. Studies in Hellenistic Civilization IV. Aarhus: Aarhus University Press.

Binford, Lewis R. 1965. "Archaeological Systematics and the Study of Culture Process," *American Antiquity* 31:203–210.

Birley, Eric (ed.). 1952. *The Congress of Roman Frontier Studies, 1949*. Registrar, University Office: University of Durham.

Blake, Emma. 1999. "Identity-Mapping in the Sardinian Bronze Age." *European Journal of Archaeology* 2:35–55.

Bloemers, J.H.F. 1983. "Acculturation in the Rhine/Meuse Basin in the Roman Period: A Preliminary Survey," in *Roman and Native in the Low Countries: Spheres of Interaction*, ed. Roel Brandt and Jan Slofstra, pp. 159–209. BAR International Series 184. Oxford: British Archaeological Reports.

_____. 1988. "Periphery in Pre- and Protohistory: Structure and Process in the Rhine-Meuse Basin between c. 600 BC and 500 AD," in *First Millennium Papers: Western Europe in the First Millennium AD*, ed. R.F.J. Jones, J.H.F. Bloemers, S.L. Dyson and M. Biddle, pp. 11–35. BAR International Series 401. Oxford: British Archaeological Reports.

_____. 1989. "Acculturation in the Rhine/Meuse Basin in the Roman Period: Some Demographic Considerations," in *Barbarians and Romans in North-West Europe: From the Later Republic to Late Antiquity*, ed. John C. Barrett, Andrew P. Fitzpatrick and Lesley Macinnes, pp. 175–197. BAR International Series 471. Oxford: British Archaeological Reports.

_____. 1991. "Relations between Romans and Natives: Concepts of Comparative Studies," in *Roman Frontier Studies 1989: Proceedings of the XVth International Congress of Roman Frontier Studies*, ed. Valerie A. Maxfield and Michael J. Dobson, pp. 451–454. Exeter: University of Exeter Press.

Boardman, Eugene P. 1965. "Chinese Mandarins and Western Traders: The Effect of the Frontier in Chinese History," in *The Frontier in Perspective*, ed. Walker D. Wyman and Clifton B. Kroeber, pp. 95–110. Madison: University of Wisconsin Press.

Bogucki, Peter. 1987. "The Establishment of Agrarian Communities on the North European Plain," *Current Anthropology* 28:1–24.

Bonzani, Renee M. 1992. "Territorial Boundaries, Buffer Zones, and Sociopolit-

Bibliography

ical Complexity: A Case Study of the Nuraghi on Sardinia," in *Sardinia in the Mediterranean: A Footprint in the Sea*, ed. Robert H. Tykot and Tamsey K. Andrews, pp. 210–220. Sheffield: Sheffield Academic Press.

Borgna, Elisabetta. 1997. "Kitchen-ware from LM IIIC Phaistos: Cooking Traditions and Ritual Activities in LBA Cretan Societies," *Studi Micenei ed Egeo-Anatolici* 39:189–217.

Branigan, Keith. 1980. "Minoan Colonialism," *Annual of the British School at Athens* 76:23–33.

_____. 1984. "Minoan Community Colonies in the Aegean," in *The Minoan Thalassocracy: Myth and Reality. Proceedings of the Third International Symposium at the Swedish Institite in Athens, 31 May–5 June 1982*, ed. Robin Hägg and Nanno Marinatos, pp. 49–52. Skrifter Utgivna av Svenska Institutet i Athen, 4, XXXII. Stockholm.

Brass, Paul R. 1991. *Ethnicity and Nationalism*. New Delhi: Sage Publications.

Braudel, Fernand. 1972. *The Mediterranean and the Mediterranean World in the Age of Philip II*. New York: Harper & Row.

Braund, David. 1984. *Rome and the Friendly King: The Character of the Client Kingship*. London: Croom Helm.

_____. 1989. "Ideology, Subsidies and Trade: The King on the Northern Frontier Revisited," in *Barbarians and Romans in North-West Europe: From the Later Republic to Late Antiquity*, ed. John C. Barrett, Andrew P. Fitzpatrick and Lesley Macinnes, pp. 14–26. BAR International Series 471. Oxford: British Archaeological Reports.

Broodbank, Cyprian. 2004. "Minoanisation." *Proceedings of the Cambridge Philosophical Society* 50:46–91.

Brown, Kenneth L. 1984. "Core or Periphery: The 'Highland Maya Question,'" in *Social and Economic Organization in the Prehispanic Andes*, ed. David L. Browman, Richard L. Burger and Mario A. Rivera, pp. 421–434. Proceedings of the International Congress of Americanists, Manchester 1982. BAR International Series 194. Oxford: British Archaeological Reports.

Buchignani, Norman. 1982. *Anthropological Approaches to the Study of Ethnicity*. Occasional Papers in Ethnic and Immigration Studies. Toronto: The Multicultural History Society of Ontario.

_____. 1987. "Ethnic Phenomena and Contemporary Social Theory: Their Implications for Archaeology," in *Ethnicity and Culture: Proceedings of the Eighteenth Annual Conference of the Archaeological Association of the University of Calgary*, ed. Reginald Auer, Margaret F. Glass, Scott McEachern and Peter H. McCarthy, pp. 15–24. Calgary: The University of Calgary Archaeological Association.

Burger, Richard L. 1984. "Archaeological Areas and Prehistoric Frontiers: The Case of Formative Peru and Ecuador," in *Social and Econonic Organization in the Prehispanic Andes*, ed. David L. Browman, Richard L. Burger and Mario A. Rivera, pp. 33–71. Proceedings of the International Congress of Americanists, Manchester 1982. BAR International Series 194. Oxford: British Archaeological Reports.

Burnham, Barry C., and John Kingsbury. 1979. "Introduction," in *Space, Hierarchy and Society: Interdisciplinary Studies in Social Area Analysis*, ed. Barry C. Burnham and John Kingsbury, pp. 4–7. BAR International Series 59. Oxford: British Archaeological Reports.

Bibliography

Bustamante, Jorge A. 1992. "Demystifying the United States-Mexico Border," *Journal of American History* 79:485–490.

Butzer, Karl W. 1988. "Diffusion, Adaptation, and Evolution of the Spanish Agrosystem," in *The Transfer and Transformation of Ideas and Material Culture*, ed. Peter J. Hugill and D. Bruce Dickson, pp. 91–109. College Station: Texas A&M University Press.

Carlisle, Susan. 1996. "Boundaries in France," in *Setting Boundaries: The Anthropology of Spatial and Social Organization*, ed. Deborah Pellow, pp. 37–54. Westport, CN: Bergin and Garvey.

Champion, Timothy C. 1989. "Introduction," in *Centre and Periphery: Comparative Studies in Archaeology*, ed. Timothy C. Champion, pp. 1–21. London: Unwin Hyman.

Chang, Claudia, and Perry A. Tourtellotte. 1993. "Ethnoarchaeological Survey of Pastoral Transhumance Sites in the Grevena Region, Greece," *Journal of Field Archaeology* 20:249–264.

Chang, Luke T. 1982. *China's Boundary Treaties and Frontier Disputes*. London: Oceana Publications, Inc.

Chapman, Graham. 1990. "Religious vs. Regional Determinism: India, Pakistan and Bangladesh as Inheritors of Empire," in *Shared Space: Divided Space: Essays on Conflict and Territorial Organization*, ed. Michael Chisholm and David M. Smith, pp. 106–134. London: Unwin Hyman.

Chappell, David A. 1993. "Ethnogenesis and Frontiers," *Journal of World History* 4: 267–275.

Chase-Dunn, Christopher, and Thomas D. Hall. 1991. "Conceptualizing Core/Periphery Hierarchies for Comparative Study," in *Core/Periphery Relations in Precapitalist Worlds*, ed. Christopher Chase-Dunn and Thomas D. Hall, pp. 5–44. Boulder: Westview Press.

Chernela, Janet M. 1992. "Social Meaning and Material Transaction: The Wanano-Tukano of Brazil and Colombia," *Journal of Anthropological Archaeology* 11:111–124.

Cherry, John F. 1987. "Power in Space: Archaeological and Geographical Studies of the State," in *Landscape and Culture: Geographical and Archaeological Perspectives*, ed. J.M. Wagstaff, pp. 146–172. Oxford: Basil Blackwell.

Cifani, Gabriele, Letizia Ceccarelli and Simon Stoddart. 2012. "Exploring a Frontier Area in Etruria: the Civita di Grotte di Castro Survey," in *Landscape, Ethnicity and Identity in the Archaic Mediterranean Area*, ed. Gabriele Cifani and Simon Stoddart, pp. 162–172. Oxford: Oxbow Books.

Clarke, David L. 1978. *Analytical Archaeology*, 2nd ed. New York: Columbia University Press.

Clarke, Simon, 1996. "Acculturation and Continuity: Re-assessing the Significance of Romanization in the Hinterlands of Gloucester and Cirencester," in *Roman Imperialism: Post-Colonial Perspectives. Proceedings of a Symposium Held at Leicester University in November 1994*, ed. Jane Webster and Nicholas J. Cooper, pp. 71–84. Leicester Archaeology Monographs No. 3. Leicester: School of Archaeological Studies, University of Leicester.

Cohen, Anthony P. 2000. "Introduction: Discriminating Relations—Identity, Boundary and Authenticity," in *Signifying Identities: Anthropological Perspectives on Boundaries and Contested Values*, ed. Anthony P. Cohen, pp. 1–13. London: Routledge.

Bibliography

Cohen, Ronald. 1978. "Ethnicity: Problem and Focus in Anthropology," *Annual Review of Anthropology* 7:379–403.

Cohen, Saul B., and Emmanuel Maier. 1983. "Partitioning and the Search for Core-Boundary Equilibrium: The Case Study of Israel," in *Ethnicity, Identity and History: Essays in Memory of Werner J. Cahnman*, ed. Joseph B. Maier and Chaim I. Waxman, pp. 291–320. London: Transaction Books.

Cohen, Yehudi. 1969. "Social Boundary Systems," *Current Anthropology* 10:103–126.

Coldstream, John Nicolas. 1993. "Mixed Marriages at the Frontiers of the Early Greek World," *Oxford Journal of Archaeology* 12:89–107.

Coles, John W., and Eric R. Wolf. 1974. *The Hidden Frontier: Ecology and Ethnicity in an Alpine Valley*. New York: Academic Press.

Cooper, Nicholas J. 1996. "Searching for the Blank Generation: Consumer Choice in Roman and Post-Roman Britain," in *Roman Imperialism: Post-Colonial Perspectives. Proceedings of a Symposium Held at Leicester University in November 1994*, ed. Jane Webster and Nicholas J. Cooper, pp. 85–98. Leicester Archaeology Monographs No. 3. Leicester: School of Archaeological Studies, University of Leicester.

Creamer, Winifred. 1984. "Evidence for Prehistoric Ethnic Groups in the Sula Valley, Honduras," in *Social and Economic Organization in the Prehispanic Andes. Proceedings of the International Congress of Americanists, Manchester 1982*, ed. David L. Browman, Richard L. Burger and Mario A. Rivera, pp. 357–384. BAR International Series 194. Oxford: British Archaeological Reports.

Cunliffe, Barry. 1988. *Greeks, Romans and Barbarians: Spheres of Interaction*. New York: Methuen.

Cusick, James G. 1998a. "Introduction," in *Studies in Culture Contact: Interaction, Culture Change, and Archaeology*, ed. James G. Cusick, pp. 1–20. Center for Archaeological Investigations, Occasional Paper No. 25. Carbondale: Southern Illinois University.

_____. 1998b. "Historiography of Acculturation: An Evaluation of Concepts and Their Application in Archaeology," in *Studies in Culture Contact: Interaction, Culture Change, and Archaeology*, ed. James G. Cusick, pp. 126–145. Center for Archaeological Investigations, Occasional Paper No. 25. Carbondale: Southern Illinois University.

D'Agata, Anna Lucia. 2000. "Interactions between Aegean Groups and Local Communities in Sicily in the Bronze Age: The Evidence from Pottery," *Studi Micenei ed Egeo-Anatolici* 42:61–83.

Daniel, Norman. 1975. *The Cultural Barrier: Problems in the Exchange of Ideas*. Edinburgh: Edinburgh University Press.

Davis, Jack L., and John Bennet. 1999. "Making Mycenaeans: Warfare, Territorial Expansion, and Representations of the Other in the Pylian Kingdom," in *Polemos: Le Contexte Guerrier en Égée à L'Âge du Bronze. Actes de la 7e Rencontre égéenne internationale, Université de Liège, 14–17 avril 1998*, ed. Robert Laffineur, pp. 105–119. Université de Liège, Histoire de l'art et archéologie de la Grèce antique/University of Texas at Austin Program in Aegean Scripts and Prehistory.

Day, Peter M., David E. Wilson and Evangelia Kiriatzi. 1998. "Pots, Labels and People: Burying Ethnicity in the Cemetery at Aghia Photia, Siteia," in *Ceme-

Bibliography

tery and Society in the Aegean Bronze Age, ed. Keith Branigan, pp. 133–149. Sheffield Studies in Aegean Archaeology 1. Sheffield: Sheffield Academic Press.

Deagan, Kathleen A. 1985. "Spanish-Indian Interaction in Sixteenth-Century Florida and Hispaniola," in *Cultures in Contact: The Impact of European Contacts on Native American Cultural Institutions, A.D. 1000–1800*, ed. William W. Fitzhugh, pp. 281–318. Anthropological Society of Washington Series. Washington, D.C.: Smithsonian Institution Press.

_____. 1998. "Transculturation and Spanish American Ethnogenesis: The Archaeological Legacy of the Quincentenary," in *Studies in Culture Contact: Interaction, Culture Change, and Archaeology*, ed. James G. Cusick, pp. 23–43. Center for Archaeological Investigations, Occasional Paper No. 25. Carbondale: Southern Illinois University.

De Atley, Suzanne P. 1984. "The Casas Grandes Frontier as a Boundary: A Case Study from Northern Mexico," in *Exploring the Limits: Frontiers and Boundaries in Prehistory*, ed. Suzanne P. De Atley and Frank J. Findlow, pp. 5–33. BAR International Series 223. Oxford: British Archaeological Reports.

DeBoer, Warren. 1981. "Buffer Zones in the Cultural Ecology of Aboriginal Amazonia: An Ethnohistorical Approach," *American Antiquity* 46:364–377.

DeCorse, Christopher R. 1989. "Material Aspects of Limba, Yalunka and Kuranko Ethnicity: Archaeological Research in Northeastern Sierra Leone," in *Archaeological Approaches to Cultural Identity*, ed. Stephen Shennan, pp. 125–140. London: Unwin Hyman.

Demarest, Arthur A. 1988. "Political Evolution in the Maya Borderlands: The Salvadoran Frontier," in *The Southeast Classic Maya Zone: A Symposium at Dumbarton Oaks, 6th and 7th October 1984*, ed. Elizabeth Hill Boone and Gordon R. Willey, pp. 335–394. Washington, D.C.: Dumbarton Oaks Research Library and Collection.

Devereux, George, and Edwin M. Loeb. 1943. "Antagonistic Acculturation," *American Sociological Review* 8:133–147.

De Vos, George A. 1995. "Ethnic Pluralism: Conflict and Accommodation," in *Ethnic Identity: Creation, Conflict and Accommodation*, 3rd ed., ed. Lola Romanucci-Ross and George DeVos, pp. 15–47. Walnut Creek, CA: Altamira Press.

Díaz-Andreu, Margarita, and Sam Lucy. 2005. "Introduction," in *The Archaeology of Identity: Approaches to Gender, Age, Status, Ethnicity, and Religion*," ed. Margarita Díaz-Andreu, Sam Lucy, Staša Babić and David N. Edwards, pp. 1–12. London: Routledge.

Dickinson, O.T.P.K. 1972. "The Shaft Graves and Mycenaean Origins," *Bulletin of the Institute of Classical Studies* 19: 146–147.

_____. 1977. *The Origins of Mycenaean Civilisation.* Studies in Mediterranean Archaeology, v. 49. Goteborg: Paul Åstroms Förlag.

_____. 1984. "Cretan Contacts with the Mainland during the Period of the Shaft Graves," in *The Minoan Thalassocracy: Myth and Reality. Proceedings of the Third International Symposium at the Swedish Institute in Athens, 31 May–5 June 1982*, ed. Robin Hägg and Nanno Marinatos, pp. 115–117. Skrifter Utgivna av Svenska Institutet i Athen, 4, XXXII. Stockholm.

Dietler, Michael. 1989. "Greeks, Etruscans, and Thirsty Barbarians: Early Iron Age Interaction in the Rhone Basin of France," in *Centre and Periphery:*

Bibliography

Comparative Studies in Archaeology, ed. Timothy C. Champion, pp. 127–141. London: Unwin Hyman.

_____. 1997. "The Iron Age in Mediterranean France: Colonial Encounters, Entanglements, and Transformations," *Journal of World Prehistory* 11: 269–353.

_____. 1998. "Consumption, Agency, and Cultural Entanglement: Theoretical Implications of a Mediterranean Colonial Encounter," in *Studies in Culture Contact: Interaction, Culture Change, and Archaeology*, ed. James G. Cusick, pp. 288–315. Center for Archaeological Investigations, Occasional Paper No. 25. Carbondale: Southern Illinois University.

_____. 2005. "The Archaeology of Colonization and the Colonization of Archaeology: Theoretical Challenges from an Ancient Mediterranean Colonial Encounter," in *The Archaeology of Colonial Encounters*, ed. Gil J. Stein, pp. 33–68. Santa Fe: School of American Research Press.

_____, and Ingrid Herbich. 1998. "*Habitus*, Techniques, Style: An Integrated Approach to the Social Understanding of Material Boundaries," in *The Archaeology of Social Boundaries*, ed. M.T. Stark, pp. 232–263. Washington, D.C.: Smithsonian Institution Press.

Dietz, Søren. 1988. "On the Origin of the Mycenaean Civilization," in *Studies in Ancient History and Numismatics Presented to Rudi Thomsen*, pp. 22–28. Aarhus: Aarhus University Press.

Dodgshon, Robert A. 1987. *The European Past: Social Evolution and Spatial Order*. London: Macmillan Education Ltd.

Dolukhanov, Pavel. 1994. *Environment and Ethnicity in the Middle East*. Aldershot: Avebury.

du Toit, Brian M. 1978. "Introduction," in *Ethnicity in Modern Africa*, ed. Brian M. du Toit, pp. 1–16. Boulder: Westview Press.

Dyson, Stephen L., 1985. *The Creation of the Roman Frontier*. Princeton: Princeton University Press.

Eadie, John. 1977. "Peripheral Vision in Roman History: Strengths and Weaknesses of the Comparative Approach," in *Ancient and Modern: Essays in Honor of Gerald F. Else*, ed. John H. D'Arms and John W. Eadie, pp. 215–234. Ann Arbor: Center for Coordination of Ancient and Modern Studies.

East, W. Gordon. 1965. *The Geography Behind History*. New York: W.W. Norton & Company.

Eccles, W.J. 1983. "Frontiers of New France," in *Essays on Frontiers in World History*, ed. George Wolfskill and Stanley Palmer, pp. 42–70. College Station: Texas A&M Press.

Eder, Birgitta. 2009. "The Northern Frontier of the Mycenaean World," in Αρχαιολογικό Έργο Θεσσαλίας και Στερεάς Ελλάδας 2 (2006). Πρακτικά Επιστημονικής Συνάντησης, Βόλος 16.3–19.3.2006, Vol. I: Θεσσαλία, ed. Alexander Mazarakis Ainian, pp. 113–131. Βόλος: Πανεπιστημίου Θεσσαλίας and Υπουργείο Πολιτισμού.

Edmonds, Richard Louis. 1985. *Northern Frontiers of Qing China and Tokugawa Japan: A Comparative Study of Frontier Policy*. University of Chicago Department of Geography Research Paper No. 213.

Eliade, Mircea. 1952. *Images and Symbols: Studies in Religious Symbolism*, trans. Philip Mairet. Princeton: Princeton University Press.

Eller, Jack and Reed Coughlan. 1993. "The Poverty of Primordialism: The Demystification of Ethnic Attachments," *Ethnic and Racial Studies* 16: 187–201.

Bibliography

Elton, Hugh. 1996. *Frontiers of the Roman Empire*. London: B T Batsford Ltd.

Enloe, Cynthia H. 1980. "Religion and Ethnicity," in *Ethnic Diversity and Conflict in Eastern Europe*, ed. Peter F. Sugar, pp. 347–371. The Joint Committee on Eastern Europe Publication Series, Number 8. Santa Barbara: ABC-Clio.

Ericksen, E. Gordon. 1980. *The Territorial Experience: Human Ecology as Symbolic Interaction*. Austin: University of Texas Press.

Ericson, Jonathon E., and Clement W. Meighan. 1984. "Boundaries, Alliance and Exchange in California," in *Exploring the Limits: Frontiers and Boundaries in Prehistory*, ed. Suzanne P. De Atley and Frank J. Findlow, pp. 143–152. BAR International Series 223. Oxford: British Archaeological Reports.

Eriksen, Thomas Hylland. 1991. "The Cultural Contexts of Ethnic Differences," *Man* 26:127–144.

Ezell, Paul H. 1961. *The Hispanic Acculturation of the Gila River Pimas*. The American Anthropological Association Memoir 90.

Febvre, Lucien. 1922. *La Terre et l'Evolution Humaine*. Paris: Renaissance du livre.

Feinman, Gary M., and Linda M. Nicholas. 1992. "Pre-Hispanic Interregional Interaction in Southern Mexico: The Valley of Oaxaca and the Ejutla Valley," in *Resources, Power and Interregional Interaction*, ed. Edward M. Schortman and Patricia A. Urban, pp. 75–116. New York: Plenum Press.

Fenton, Steve. 2003. *Ethnicity*. Cambridge: Polity Press.

Ferguson, R. Brian, and Neil L. Whitehead (eds.). 1992. *War in the Tribal Zone: Expanding States and Indigenous Warfare*. Santa Fe: School of American Research Press.

Fernandez, James W. 2000. "Peripheral Wisdom," in *Signifying Identities: Anthropological Perspectives on Boundaries and Contested Values*, ed. Anthony P. Cohen, pp. 117–144. London: Routledge.

Feuer, Bryan. 1983. *The Northern Mycenaean Border in Thessaly*. BAR International Series 176. Oxford: British Archaeological Reports.

_____. 1994. "Mycenaean Thessaly," in *La Thessalie: Quinze annes de Recherche archéologiques, 1975–1990, Bilans et Perspectives. Actes du Colloque International, Lyon, 17–22 Avril 1990*, pp. 211–214. Athens: Kapon Press.

_____. 1999. 'The Mycenaean Periphery: Some Theoretical and Methodological Considerations," in *First International Interdisciplinary Colloquium: The Periphery of the Mycenaean World, 25–29 September, Lamia 1994*, pp. 7–14. Lamia: 14th Ephorate of Prehistoric and Classical Antiquities.

_____. 2003. "Cultural Interaction Processes in the Mycenaean Periphery," in N. Kyparissi-Apostolika and M. Papakonstantinou (eds), *2nd International Interdisciplinary Colloquium: The Periphery of the Mycenaean World, 26–30 September, Lamia 1999*, pp. 15–24. Athens: Ministry of Culture, 14th Ephorate of Prehistoric and Classical Antiquities.

_____. 2004. *Mycenaean Civilization: An Annotated Bibliography, Through 2002*. Revised Edition. Jefferson, NC: McFarland.

_____. 2011. "Being Mycenaean: A View from the Periphery," *American Journal of Archaeology* 115:507–536.

_____. 2014. "Environmental Aspects of the Northern Mycenaean Border in Thessaly," in *PHYSIS: L'environnement Naturel et la Relation Homme-milieu dans le Monde égéen protohistorique. Actes de la 14e Rencontre égéenne interna-*

Bibliography

tionale, Paris, Institut National d'Histoire de l'Art (INHA), 11–14 décembre 2012, ed. Gilles Touchais, Robert Laffineur and Françoise Rougemont, p.473. Leuven-Liege: Peeters.

_____. 2015. "Mycenaeanisation in Thessaly, A Study in Differential Acculturation," in *Beyond Thalassocracies. Understanding Processes of Minoanisation and Mycenaeanisation in the Aegean*, ed. Evi Gorogianni, Peter Pavúk, and Luca Girella. Oxford: Oxbow Books.

_____. 2016. "Modeling Differential Cultural Interaction in Late Bronze Age Thessaly," in *What Happened on the Fringe: Testing a New Model of Cross-Cultural Interaction in Ancient Borderlands*, ed. Ulrike Matthies Green and Kirk E. Costion. Gainesville: University Press of Florida.

_____, and Gerwulf Schneider. 2003. "Chemical Analysis and Interpretation of Mycenaean Pottery from Thessaly," *Journal of Mediterranean Archaeology* 16: 217–247.

Finkelstein, Israel. 1995. *Living on the Fringe: The Archaeology and History of the Negev, Sinai and Neighbouring Regions in the Bronze and Iron Ages*. Sheffield: Sheffield Academic Press.

Fischer, Eric. 1949. "On Boundaries," *World Politics* 1:196–222.

Forbes, Jack D. 1968. "Frontiers in American History and the Role of the Frontier Historian," *Ethnohistory* 15:203–235.

Foster, George M. 1960. *Culture and Conquest: America's Spanish Heritage*. Viking Fund Publications in Anthropology No. 27. Chicago: Quadrangle Books.

Foster, Michael S. 1986. "The Mesoamerican Connection: A View from the South," in *Ripples in the Chichimec Sea: New Considerations of Southwestern-Mesoamerican Interactions*, ed. Frances Joan Mathien and Randall H. McGuire, pp. 55–69. Carbondale: Southern Illinois University Press.

Franklin, Natalie R. 1989. "Research With Style: A Case Study from Australian Rock Art," in *Archaeological Approaches to Cultural Identity*, ed. Stephen Shennan, pp. 278–290. London: Unwin Hyman.

Fulford, Michael F. 1985. "Roman Material in Barbarian Society c. 200 B.C.-c. A.D. 400, in *Settlement and Society: Aspects of West European Prehistory in the First Millennium B.C.*, ed. T.C. Champion and J.V.S. Megaw, pp. 91–108. New York: St. Martin's Press.

_____. 1989. "Roman and Barbarian: The Economy of Roman Frontier Systems," in *Barbarians and Romans in North-West Europe: From the Later Republic to Late Antiquity*, ed. John C. Barrett, Andrew P. Fitzpatrick and Lesley Macinnes, pp. 81–95. BAR International Series 471, Oxford: British Archaeological Reports.

Galaty, John G. 1993. "'The Eye that Wants a Person, Where Can It Not See?': Inclusion, Exclusion and Boundary Shifters in Maasai Identity," in *Being Maasai: Ethnicity & Identity in East Africa*, ed. Thomas Spear and Richard Walker, pp. 174–194. London: James Currey.

Galaty, Michael L., and William A. Parkinson. 2007. "Introduction," in *Rethinking Mycenaean Palaces II*, 2nd rev. ed., ed. Michael L. Galaty and William A. Parkinson, pp. 1–17. Cotsen Institute of Archaeology Monograph 60. Los Angeles: Cotsen Institute of Archaeology.

Galtung, Johan. 1972. "Eine Strukturelle Theorie des Imperialismus," in *Imperialismus und Strukturelle Gewalt: Analysen uber abhaginge Reproduktion*, ed. D. Senghaas, pp. 19–104. Frankfurt: Suhrkamp.

Bibliography

Garcia-Arevalo, Manuel. 1989. "Transculturation in Contact Period and Contemporary Hispaniola," in *Columbian Consequences, Volume 2: Archaeological and Historical Perspectives on the Spanish Borderlands East*, ed. David
Hurst Thomas, pp. 269–280. Washington, D.C.: Smithsonian Institution
Press.

Gerhard, Dietrich. 1959. "The Frontier in Comparative View," *Comparative Studies in Society and History* 1:205–229.

Gerstle, Andrea I. 1984. "Ethnic Diversity and Interaction at Copan, Honduras,"
in *Social and Economic Organization in the Prehispanic Andes*, ed. David
L. Browman, Richard L. Burger and Mario A. Rivera, pp. 328–356. Proceedings of the International Congress of Americanists, Manchester 1982.
BAR International Series 194. Oxford: British Archaeological Reports.

Gibson, D. Blair. 1988. "Agro-Pastoralism and Regional Social Organization in
Early Ireland," in *Tribe and Polity in Late Prehistoric Europe: Demography,
Production, and Exchange in the Evolution of Complex Social Systems*, ed.
D. Blair Gibson and Michael N. Geselowitz, pp. 41–68. New York: Plenum
Press.

Giddens, Anthony, Franciszek Ociepka, and Wiktor Zujewicz. 1973. *The Class
Structure of the Advanced Societies*. London: Hutchinson.

Gosden, Chris. 2004. *Archaeology and Colonialism: Cultural Contact from 5000
BC to the Present*. Cambridge: Cambridge University Press.

Gosselain, Olivier P. 2000. "Materializing Identities: an African Perspective,"
Journal of Archaeological Method and Theory 7:187–217.

Gottmann, Jean. 1973. *The Significance of Territory*. Charlottesville: The University Press of Virginia.

_____. 1980. "Confronting Centre and Periphery," in *Centre and Periphery: Spatial
Variation in Politics*, ed. Jean Gottman, pp. 11–25. Beverly Hills: Sage Publications.

Goudriaan, Koen. 1988. *Ethnicity in Ptolemaic Egypt*. Dutch Monographs on
Ancient History and Archaeology, Volume V. Amsterdam: J.C. Gieben.

_____. 1992. "Ethnical Strategies in Graeco-Roman Egypt," in *Ethnicity in Hel-
lenistic Egypt*, ed. Per Bilde, Troels Engberg-Pedersen, Lise Hannestad and
Jan Zahle, pp. 74–99. Studies in Hellenistic Civilization III. Aarhus: Aarhus
University Press.

Grahame, Mark. 1998. "Rome without Romanization: Cultural Change in the
Pre-Desert of Tripolitania (First-Third Centuries AD)," *Oxford Journal of
Archaeology* 17:93–111.

Graner, G., and L. Karlenby. 2007. "Keeping Up Appearances: On the Northern
Frontier in Scandinavian Funnel Beaker Times," in *Encounters / Materialities /
Confrontations: Archaeologies of Social Space and Interaction*, ed. P. Cornell
and F. Fahlander, pp. 150–164. Newcastle: Cambridge Scholars Press.

Green, Stanton W. 1979. "The Agricultural Colonization of Temperate Forest
Habitats: An Ecological Model, in *The Frontier: Comparative Studies, Vol-
ume Two*, ed. William W. Savage, Jr. and Stephen I. Thompson, pp. 69–103.
Norman: University of Oklahoma Press.

Green, Ulrike, and Kirk E. Costion. 2016. *What Happened on the Fringe: Testing
a New Model of Cross-Cultural Interaction in Ancient Borderlands*.
Gainesville: University Press of Florida.

Gregg, Susan Alling. 1988. *Foragers and Farmers: Population Interaction and*

Bibliography

Agricultural Expansion in Prehistoric Europe. Chicago: The University of Chicago Press.

Groenman-van Waateringe, W. 1980. "Urbanization and the North-West Frontier of the Roman Empire," in *Roman Frontier Studies 1979; Papers Presented to the 12th International Congress of Roman Studies*, ed. W.S. Hanson and L.J.E. Keppie, pp. 1037–1044. BAR International Series 71. Oxford: British Archaeological Reports.

_____. 1983. "The Disastrous Effect of the Roman Occupation," in *Roman and Native in the Low Countries: Spheres of Interaction*, ed. Roel Brandt and Jan Slofstra, pp. 147–157. BAR International Series 184, Oxford: British Archaeological Reports.

Grosby, Steven. 1994. "The Verdict of History: The Inexpungeable Tie of Primordiality—A Response to Eller and Coughlin," *Ethnic and Racial Studies* 17: 164–171.

Guillotte, Joseph V. III. 1978. "Citizens and Tribesmen: Variations in Ethnic Affiliation in a Multiethnic Farming Community in Northern Tanzania," in *Ethnicity in Modern Africa*, ed. Brian M. du Toit, ed., pp. 19–46. Boulder: Westview Press.

Guy, Donna J., and Thomas E. Sheridan. 1998. *Contested Ground: Comparative Frontiers on the Northern and Southern Edges of the Spanish Empire.* Tucson: University of Arizona Press.

Haefeli, Evan. 1999. "A Note on the Use of North American Borderlands," *American Historical Review* 104:1222–1225.

Hägg, Robin. 1982. "On the Nature of Minoan Influence in Early Mycenaean Messenia," *Opuscula Atheniensia* 14: 7–37.

Hall, Edith. 1989. *Inventing the Barbarian: Greek Self-Definition through Tragedy.* Oxford: Clarendon Press.

Hall, Jonathan M. 1997. *Ethnic Identity in Greek Antiquity.* Cambridge: Cambridge University Press.

Hall, Thomas D. 1991. "The Role of Nomads in Core/Periphery Relations," in *Core/Periphery Relations in Precapitalist Worlds*, ed. Christopher Chase-Dunn and Thomas D. Hall, pp. 212–239. Boulder: Westview Press.

_____. 1998. "The Río de la Plata and the Greater Southwest: A View from World-System Theory," in *Contested Ground: Comparative Frontiers on the Northern and Southern Edges of the Spanish Empire*, ed. D.J. Guy and T.E. Sheridan, pp. 150–166. Tucson: University of Arizona Press.

_____. 2000. "Frontiers, Ethnogenesis, and World-Systems: Rethinking the Theories," in *A World-Systems Reader: New Perspectives on Gender, Urbanism, Cultures, Indigenous Peoples and Ecology*, ed. Thomas D. Hall, pp. 237–270. Lanham, MD: Rowman & Littlefield.

Hanson, W.S. 1989. "The Nature and Function of Roman Frontiers," in *Barbarians and Romans in North-West Europe: From the Later Republic to Late Antiquity*, ed. John C. Barrett, Andrew P. Fitzpatrick and Lesley Macinnes, pp. 55–63. BAR International Series 471. Oxford: British Archaeological Reports.

_____, and L.J.E. Keppie (eds.). 1980. *Roman Frontier Studies 1979; Papers Presented to the 12th International Congress of Roman Studies.* BAR International Series 71. Oxford: British Archaeological Reports.

Harrell, Stevan. 1990. "Ethnicity, Local Interests, and the State: Yi Communities

Bibliography

in Southwest China," *Comparative Studies in Society and History* 32:515–548.

_____. 1995. "Languages Defining Ethnicity in Southwest China," in *Ethnic Identity: Creation, Conflict and Accommodation*, 3rd ed., ed. Lola Romanucci-Ross and George DeVos, pp. 97–114. Walnut Creek: Altamira Press.

Hartshorne, Richard. 1936. "Suggestions on the Terminology of Political Boundaries," *Annals of the Association of American Geographers* 26:56–57.

Haselgrove, Colin. 1984. "'Romanization' Before the Conquest: Gaulish Precedents and British Consequences," in *Military and Civilian in Roman Britain: Cultural Relationships in a Frontier Province*, ed. T.F.C. Blagg and A.C. King, pp. 5–63. BAR British Series 136. Oxford: British Archaeological Reports.

_____. 1990. "The Romanization of Belgic Gaul: Some Archaeological Perspectives," in *The Early Roman Empire in the West*, ed. Thomas Blagg and Martin Millett, pp. 45–71. Oxford: Oxbow Books.

Hedeager, Lotte. 1979. "A Quantitative Analysis of Roman Imports in Europe North of the Limes (0–400 A.D.), and the Question of Roman-Germanic Exchange," in *New Directions in Scandinavian Archaeology*, ed. Kristian Kristiansen and Carsten Paludan-Muller, pp. 191–216. Studies in Scandanavian Prehistory and Early History, Volume 1. Copenhagen: The National Museum of Denmark.

_____. 1987. "Empire, Frontier and the Barbarian Hinterland: Rome and Northern Europe from AD 1–400," in *Center and Periphery in the Ancient World*, ed. Michael Rowlands, Mogens Larsen and Kristian Kristiansen, pp. 125–140. Cambridge: Cambridge University Press.

Hegmon, M. 1998. "Technology, Style, and Social Practices: Archaeological Approaches," in *The Archaeology of Social Boundaries*, ed. Miriam T. Stark, pp. 264–279. Washington, D.C.: Smithsonian Institution Press.

Helms, Mary. 1988. *Ulysses' Sail: An Ethnographic Odyssey of Power, Knowledge, and Geographical Distance*. Princeton: Princeton University Press.

Hennessy, Alistair. 1978. *The Frontier in Latin American History*. Albuquerque: University of New Mexico Press.

Herskovits, Melville J. 1967. *Cultural Dynamics*, New York: Alfred A. Knopf.

Hickerson, Harold. 1965. "The Virginia Deer and Intertribal Buffer Zones in the Upper Mississippi Valley," in *Man, Culture, and Animals: The Role of Animals in Human Ecological Adjustments*, ed. Anthony Leeds and Andrew P. Vayda, pp. 43–65. American Association for the Advancement of Science, Publication No. 78. Washington, D.C.

Higginbotham, Carolyn R. 2000. *Egyptianization and Elite Emulation in Ramesside Palestine: Governance and Accommodation on the Imperial Periphery*. Culture and History of the Ancient Near East, Vol. 2. Leiden: Brill.

Higham, N.J. 1989. "Roman and Native in England North of the Tees: Acculturation and its Limitations," in *Barbarians and Romans in North-West Europe: From the Later Republic to Late Antiquity*, ed. John C. Barrett, Andrew P. Fitzpatrick and Lesley Macinnes, pp. 153–174. BAR International Series 471. Oxford: British Archaeological Reports.

Hill, Carol W. 1989. "Who is What? A Preliminary Enquiry into Cultural and Physical Identity," in *Archaeological Approaches to Cultural Identity*, ed. Stephen Shennan, pp. 233–241. London: Unwin Hyman.

Bibliography

Hingely, Richard. 1996. "The 'Legacy' of Rome: The Rise, Decline and Fall of the Theory of Romanization," in *Roman Imperialism: Post-Colonial Perspectives. Proceedings of a Symposium Held at Leicester University in November 1994*, ed. Jane Webster and Nicholas J. Cooper, pp. 35–48. Leicester Archaeology Monographs No. 3. Leicester: School of Archaeological Studies, University of Leicester.

Hirth, Kenneth G. 1978. "Interregional Trade and the Formation of Prehistoric Gateway Communities," *American Antiquity* 43:35–45.

Hodder, Ian. 1979. "Economic and Social Stress and Material Culture Patterning," *American Antiquity* 44:446–454.

_____. 1982. *Symbols in Action: Ethnoarchaeological Studies of Material Culture.* Cambridge: Cambridge University Press.

_____, and Clive Orton. 1976. *Spatial Analysis in Archaeology.* Cambridge: Cambridge University Press.

Hodgson, Nicholas. 1989. "The East as Part of the Wider Roman Imperial Frontier Policy," in *The Eastern Frontier of the Roman Empire: Proceedings of a Colloquium Held at Ankara in September 1988*, eds. D.H. French and C.S. Lightfoot, pp. 177–189. British Institute of Archaeology at Ankara Monograph No. 11. BAR International Series 553. Oxford: British Archaeological Reports.

Hodos, Tamar. 2006. *Local Responses to Colonization in the Iron Age Mediterranean.* London: Routledge.

_____. 2009. "Colonial Engagements in the Global Mediterranean Iron Age." *Cambridge Archaeological Journal* 19:221–241.

Horden, Perigrine, and Nicholas Purcell. 2000. *The Corrupting Sea: A Study of Mediterranean History.* Oxford: Blackwell.

Horowitz, Donald L. 1975. "Ethnic Identity," in *Ethnicity: Theory and Experience*, ed. Nathan Glazer and Daniel P. Moynihan, pp. 111–140. Cambridge, MA: Harvard University Press.

Howard, Alan. 1990. "Cultural Paradigms, History, and the Search for Identity in Oceania," in *Cultural Identity and Ethnicity in the Pacific*, ed. Jocelyn Linnekin and Lin Poyer, pp. 259–279. Honolulu: University of Hawaii Press.

Hudson, John C. 1977. "Theory and Methodology in Comparative Frontier Studies," in *The Frontier: Comparative Studies*, ed. David Harry Miller, pp. 11–31. Norman: University of Oklahoma Press.

Hugill, Peter J., and D. Bruce Dickson. 1988. *The Transfer and Transformation of Ideas and Material Culture.* College Station: Texas A&M Press.

Hutchinson, J., and A.D. Smith. 1996. "Introduction," in *Ethnicity*, ed. J. Hutchinson and A.D. Smith, pp. 3–16. Oxford: Oxford University Press.

Jones, Siân. 1996. "Discourses of Identity in the Interpretation of the Past," in *Cultural Identity and Archaeology: The Construction of European Communities*, ed. Paul Graves-Brown, Siân Jones and Clive Gamble, pp. 62–80. London: Routledge.

_____. 1997. *The Archaeology of Ethnicity: Constructing Identities in the Past and Present.* London: Routledge.

Kamp, Kathryn A., and Norman Yoffee. 1980. "Ethnicity in Ancient Western Asia during the Early Second Millennium B.C.: Archaeological Assessments and Ethnoarchaeological Prospectives," *Bulletin of the American Schools of Oriental Research* 237: 85–104.

Bibliography

Kapil, Ravi L. 1966. "On the Conflict of Inherited Boundaries in Africa," *World Politics* 18:656–673.

Kardulias, P. Nick. 1999. "Preface," in *World Systems Theory and Practice: Leadership, Production, and Exchange*, ed. P.N. Kardulias, pp. xvii–xxi. Lanham, MD: Rowman and Littlefield.

Katz, Elihu, Martin L. Levin and Herbert Hamilton. 1963. "Traditions of Research on the Diffusion of Innovation," *American Sociological Review* 28:237–252.

Keyes, Charles F. 1981. "The Dialectics of Ethnic Change," in *Ethnic Change*, ed. Charles F. Keyes, pp. 4–30. Seattle: University of Washington Press.

Kilian, Klaus. 1990. "Mycenaean Colonization: Norm and Variety," in *Greek Colonists and Native Populations: Proceedings of the First Australian Congress of Classical Archaeology held in Honour of Emeritus Professor A.D. Trendall, Sidney, 9–14 July 1985*, ed. Jean-Paul Descoeudres, pp. 445–467. Humanities Research Centre, Canberra. Oxford: Clarendon Press.

Kimes, T., Colin Haselgrove and Ian Hodder. 1982. "A Method for the Identification of the Location of Regional Cultural Boundaries," *Journal of Anthropological Archaeology* 1:113–131.

King, Anthony C. 1984. "Animal Bones and the Dietary Identity of Military and Civilian Groups in Roman Britain, Germany and Gaul," in *Military and Civilian in Roman Britain: Cultural Relationships in a Frontier Province*, ed. T.F.C. Blagg and A.C. King, pp. 187–217. BAR British Series 136. Oxford: British Archaeological Reports.

Kiriatzi, Evangelia. 2000. "Pottery Technologies and People at LBA Toumba Thessalonikis," *Bulletin of the Institute of Classical Studies* 44:222.

Kohl, Philip L. 1987. "The Ancient Economy, Transferable Technologies and the Bronze Age World-System: A View from the Northeastern Frontier of the Ancient Near East," in *Center and Periphery in the Ancient World*, ed. Michael Rowlands, Mogens Larsen and Kristian Kristiansen, pp. 13–24. Cambridge: Cambridge University Press.

_____. 1989. "The Transcaucasian 'Periphery' in the Bronze Age," in *Resources, Power and Interregional Interaction*, ed. Edward M. Schortman and Patricia A. Urban, pp. 117–137. New York: Plenum Press.

Kolchin, Peter. 1982. "Comparing American History," *Reviews in American History* 10:64–81.

Kopytoff, Igor. 1987. "The Internal African Frontier: The Making of African Political Culture," in *The African Frontier: The Reproduction of Traditional African Societies*, ed. Igor Kopytoff, pp. 3–84. Bloomington: Indiana University Press.

Kowalewski, Stephen A., Richard E. Blanton, Gary Feinman and Laura Finsten. 1983. "Boundaries, Scale, and Internal Organization." *Journal of Anthropological Archaeology* 2:32–56.

Kratochwil, Friedrich. 1986. "Of Systems, Boundaries, and Territoriality: An Inquiry into the Formation of the State System," *World Politics* 39:27–52.

Kristiansen, Kristian, and Thomas B. Larsson. 2005. *The Rise of Bronze Age Society: Travels, Transmissions and Transformations*. Cambridge: Cambridge University Press.

Kristof, Ladis K.D. 1959. "The Nature of Frontiers and Boundaries," *Annals of the Association of American Geographers* 49–269–282.

Kunstadter, Peter. 1967. "Introduction," in *Southeast Asian Tribes, Minorities,*

Bibliography

and Nations, Vol. 1, ed. Peter Kunstadter, pp. 3–72. Princeton: Princeton University Press.

Kurchin, Bernice. 1995. "Romans and Britons on the Northern Frontier: A Theoretical Evaluation of the Archaeology of Resistance," in *Theoretical Roman Archaeology: Second Conference Proceedings*, ed. Peter Rush, pp. 124–140. Aldershot: Avebury.

Laffineur, Robert (ed.). 1989. *Transition: Le Monde égéene du Bronze Moyen au Bronze Récent. Actes de la deuxié Rencontre égéene internationale de l'Université de Liège (18–20 avril 1988)*. Aegaeum 3, Annales d'archéologie égéene de l'Université de Liège. Liège: Université de l'Etat à Liège.

Larsson, Thomas B. 1988. "A Spatial Approach to Socioeconomic Change in Scandinavia: Central Sweden in the First Millennium B.C.," in *Tribe and Polity in Late Prehistoric Europe: Demography, Production, and Exchange in the Evolution of Complex Social Systems*, ed. D. Blair Gibson and Michael N. Geselowitz, pp. 97–115. New York: Plenum Press.

Lattimore, Owen. 1962. *Studies in Frontier History*. London: Oxford University Press.

_____. 1979. "Geography and the Ancient Empires," in *Power and Propaganda: A Symposium on Ancient Empires*, ed. Mogens Trolle Larsen, pp. 35–41. Copenhagen Studies in Assyriology, v. 7. Copenhagen: Akademisk Forlag.

_____. 1980. "The Periphery as a Locus of Innovation," in *Centre and Periphery: Spatial Variation in Politics*, ed. Jean Gottman, pp. 205–208. Beverly Hills: Sage Publications.

Leach, Edmund. 1960. "The Frontiers of 'Burma,'" *Comparative Studies in Society and History* 3:49–68.

Lee, Robert H. G. 1970. *The Manchurian Frontier in Ch'ing History*. Cambridge: Harvard University Press.

Lerner, Shereen. 1984. "Defining Prehistoric Frontiers: A Methodological Approach," in *Exploring the Limits: Frontiers and Boundaries in Prehistory*, ed. Suzanne P. De Atley and Frank J. Findlow, pp. 67–80. BAR International Series 223, Oxford: British Archaeological Reports.

_____. 1987. "An Application of a Core-Periphery Model to Prehistoric Societies in Central Arizona," in *Polities and Partitions: Human Boundaries and the Growth of Complex Societies*, ed. Kathryn Maurer Trinkaus, pp. 97–121. Arizona State University Anthropological Research Papers No. 39.

Leventhal, Richard M., Arthur A. Demarest and Gordon R. Willey. 1987. "The Cultural and Social Components of Copan," in *Polities and Partitions: Human Boundaries and the Growth of Complex Societies*, ed. Kathryn Maurer Trinkaus, pp. 179–205. Arizona State University Anthropological Research Papers No.37.

Lewis, Archibald R. 1958. "The Closing of the Medieval Frontier, 1250–1350," *Speculum* 33:475–483.

Lewis, Kenneth E. 1977. "Sampling the Archaeological Frontier: Regional Models and Component Analysis," in *Research Strategies in Historical Archaeology*, ed. Stanley South, pp. 151–201. New York: Academic Press.

_____. 1984. *The American Frontier: An Archaeological Study of Settlement Pattern and Process*. Orlando: Academic Press.

Lightfoot, Kent G., and Antoinette Martinez. 1995. "Frontiers and Boundaries in Archaeological Perspective," *Annual Review of Anthropology* 24:471–492.

Bibliography

Linnekin, Jocelyn, and Lin Poyer. 1990. "Introduction," in *Cultural Identity and Ethnicity in the Pacific*, ed. Jocelyn Linnekin and Lin Poyer, pp. 1–16. Honolulu: University of Hawaii Press.

Linton, Ralph. 1936. *The Study of Man: An Introduction*. London: Appleton-Century-Crofts.

Liverani, Mario. 1987. "The Collapse of the Near Eastern Regional System at the End of the Bronze Age: The Case of Syria," in *Center and Periphery in the Ancient World*, ed. Michael Rowlands, Mogens Larsen and Kristian Kristiansen, pp. 66–73. Cambridge: Cambridge University Press.

Luraghi, Nino, 2008. *The Ancient Messenians: Constructions of Ethnicity and Memory*. Cambridge: Cambridge University Press.

Macbeth, Helen. 1993. "Ethnicity and Human Biology," in *Social and Biological Aspects of Ethnicity*, ed. Malcolm Chapman, pp. 47–91. Oxford: Oxford University Press.

MacEachern, Scott. 1998. "Technological Traditions in the Northern Mandara Mountains," in *The Archaeology of Social Boundaries*, ed. Miriam T. Stark, pp. 107–131. Washington, D.C.: Smithsonian Institution Press.

Mac Sweeney, Naoíse. 2009. "Beyond Ethnicity: The Overlooked Diversity of Group Identities," *Journal of Mediterranean Archaeology* 22:101–126.

Malkin, Irad. 2002. "A Colonial Middle Ground: Greek, Etruscan and Local Elites in the Bay of Naples," in *The Archaeology of Colonialism*, ed. C.L. Lyons and J.K. Papadopoulos, pp. 151–181. Los Angeles: Getty Research Institute.

Malmberg, Torsten. 1980. *Human Territoriality*. The Hague: Mouton.

Maran, Joseph. 1992. *Die deutschen Ausgrabungen auf der Pevkakia-Magoula in thessalien. III. Die mittlere Bronzezeit*, Bonn: Habelt.

_____. 1995. "Structural Changes in the Pattern of Settlement during the Shaft Grave Period on the Greek Mainland," in *Politeia: Society and State in the Aegean Bronze Age: Proceedings of the 5th International Aegean Conference, University of Heidelberg, Archaologisches Institut, 10–13 April 1994*, ed. Robert Laffineur and Wolf-Dietrich Niemeier, pp. 67–72. Annales d'archéologie égéenne de l'Université de Liège et UT-PASP. Liège, Université de Liège, Histoire de l'art et archéologie de la Grece antique/University of Texas at Austin, Program in Aegean Scripts and Prehistory.

Marotta, Vince P. 2008. "The Hybrid Self and the Ambivalence of Boundaries," *Social Identities* 14: 295–312.

Martinez, Oscar J. 1988. *Troublesome Border*. Tucson: University of Arizona Press.

Mattingly, David. 2010. "Cultural Crossovers: Global and Local Identities in the Classical World," in *Material Culture and Social Identities in the Ancient World*, ed. Shelley Hales and Tamar Hodos, pp. 283–295. Cambridge: Cambridge University Press.

Maxfield, Valerie A., and Michael J. Dobson (eds.). 1991. *Roman Frontier Studies 1989: Proceedings of the XVth International Congress of Roman Frontier Studies*. Exeter: University of Exeter Press.

McGuire, Randall H. 1982. "The Study of Ethnicity in Historical Archaeology," *Journal of Anthropological Archaeology* 1: 159–178.

_____. 1986. "Economies and Modes of Production in the Prehistoric Southwestern Periphery," in *Ripples in the Chichimec Sea: New Considerations of Southwestern-Mesoamerican Interactions*, ed. Frances Joan Mathien and

Bibliography

Randall H. McGuire, pp. 243–269. Carbondale: Southern Illinois University Press.

_____. 1989. "The Greater Southwest as a Periphery of Mesoamerica," in *Centre and Periphery: Comparative Studies in Archaeology*, ed. Timothy C. Champion, pp. 40–66. London: Unwin Hyman.

Mckee, Larry W. 1987. "Delineating Ethnicity from the Garbage of Early Virginians: Faunal Remains from the Kingsmill Plantation Slave Quarter," *American Archaeology* 6:31–39.

Melas, Manolis. 1988. "Minoans Overseas: Alternative Models of Interpretation," in *Aegaeum 2, Annales d'archéologie égéenne de l'Université de Liège, Université de l'Etat à Liège, Histoire de l'art et archéologie de la Grèce antique*, pp. 47–70. Liège.

Mellor, Roy E.H. 1989. *Nation, State, and Territory: A Political Geography*. London: Routledge.

Mikesell, Marvin W. 1968. "Comparative Studies in Frontier History," in *Turner and the Sociology of the Frontier*, ed. Richard Hofstadter and Seymour Martin Lipset, pp. 152–174. New York: Basic Books, Inc.

Milojčić, Vladimir. 1955. "Vorbericht über die Ausgrabungen auf den Magulen Von Otzaki, Arapi und Gremnos bei Larisa 1955," *Archäologischer Anzeiger* 70:182–231.

Millar, Fergus, D. Berciu, Richard N. Frye, Georg Kossack and Tamara Talbot Rice. 1967. *The Roman Empire and its Neighbours*. Delacorte World History, Vol. VIII. New York: Delacorte Press,

Miller, David Harry. 1996. "Frontier Societies and the Transition Between Late Antiquity and the Early Middle Ages, in *Shifting Frontiers in Late Antiquity*, ed. Ralph W. Mathison and Hagith S. Sivan, pp. 158–171. Aldershot: Variorum.

Millett, Martin. 1970. *The Romanization of Britain: An Essay in Archaeological Interpretation*. Cambridge: Cambridge University Press.

_____. 1990. "Romanization: Historical Issues and Archaeological Interpretation," in *The Early Roman Empire in the West*, ed. Thomas Blagg and Martin Millett, pp. 35–44, Oxford: Oxbow Books.

Moerman, Michael. 1965. "Ethnic Identification in a Complex Civilization: Who Are the Lue?" *American Anthropologist* 67:1215–1230.

Monroe, J.C. 2002. *Negotiating African-American Ethnicity in the 17th Century Chesapeake: Colono Tobacco Pipes and the Ethnic Uses of Style*. The Archaeology of the Clay Tobacco Pipe XVI. BAR International Series 1042. Oxford: Archaeopress.

Motyl, Alexander J. 2001. *Imperial Ends: The Decay, Collapse and Revival of Empires*, New York: Columbia University Press.

Mountjoy, Penelope A. 1999. *Regional Mycenaean Decorated Pottery*. Rahden/Westfalia: Verlag Marie Leidorf GmbH.

Nagata, Judith. 1981. "In Defense of Ethnic Boundaries: The Changing Myths and Charters of Malay Identity," in *Ethnic Change*, ed. Charles F. Keyes, pp. 88–116. Seattle: University of Washington Press.

Naroll, Raoul. 1964. "On Ethnic Unit Classification," *Current Anthropology* 5:283–312.

Nash, Daphne. 1985. "Celtic Territorial Expansion and the Mediterranean World," in *Settlement and Society: Aspects of West European Prehistory in the First*

Bibliography

Millennium B.C., ed. T.C. Champion and J.V.S. Megaw, pp. 45–67. New York: St. Martin's Press.

Nash, Manning. 1989. *The Cauldron of Ethnicity in the Modern World*. Chicago: University of Chicago Press.

Nelson, Ben A. 1993. "Outposts of Mesoamerican Empire and Architectural Patterning at La Quemada, Zacatecas," in *Culture and Contact: Charles C. Di Peso's Gran Chichimeca*, ed. Anne I. Woosely and John C. Ravesloot, pp. 173–189. Albuquerque: University of New Mexico Press.

Newby, Gordon D. 1983. "Ibn Khaldun and Frederick Jackson Turner: Islam and the Frontier Experience," *Journal of Asian and African Studies* 18:274–285.

Okey, Robin. 1992. "Central Europe / Eastern Europe: Behind the Definitions," *Past and Present* 137: 102–133.

Okun, Marcia L. 1989. *The Early Roman Frontier in the Upper Rhine Area: Assimilation and Acculturation on a Roman Frontier*. BAR International Series 547. Oxford: British Archaeological Reports.

Osborne, Robin. 1987. *Classical Landscape with Figures: The Ancient Greek City and its Countryside*. London: George Philip.

Ostergard, Uffe. 1992. "What is National and Ethnic Identity?" in *Ethnicity in Hellenistic Egypt*, ed. Per Bilde, Troels Engberg-Pedersen, Lise Hannestad and Jan Zahle, pp. 16–38. Studies in Hellenistic Civilization III. Aarhus: Aarhus University Press.

Owsley, Frank L. 1945. "The Pattern of Migration and Settlement on the Southern Frontier," *The Journal of Southern History* 11:147–176.

Pailes, Richard A. and Daniel T. Reff. 1985. "Colonial Exchange Systems and the Decline of Paquime," in *The Archaeology of West and Northwest Mesoamerica*, ed. Michael S. Foster and Phil C. Weigand, pp. 353–363. Boulder: Westview Press.

Pantou, Panagiota A. 2010. "Mycenaean Dimini in Context: Investigating Regional Variability and Socioeconomic Complexities in Late Bronze Age Greece," *American Journal of Archaeology* 114:381–401.

Parker, Bradley J. 2006. "Toward an Understanding of Borderland Processes," *American Antiquity* 71:77–100.

Parker Pearson, Michael. 1989. "Beyond the Pale: Barbarian Social Dynamics in Western Europe," in *Barbarians and Romans in North-West Europe: From the Later Republic to Late Antiquity*, ed. John C. Barrett, Andrew P. Fitzpatrick and Lesley Macinnes, pp. 198–226. BAR International Series 471. Oxford: British Archaeological Reports.

Parkinson, William A. 2006. "Tribal Boundaries: Stylistic Variability and Social Boundary Maintenance during the Transition to the Copper Age on the Great Hungarian Plain," *Journal of Anthropological Archaeology* 25: 33–58.

Patterson, Orlando. 1975. "Context and Choice in Ethnic Allegiance: A Theoretical Framework and Caribbean Case Study," in *Ethnicity: Theory and Experience*, ed. Nathan Glazer and Daniel P. Moynihan, pp. 305–349. Cambridge, MA: Harvard University Press.

_____. 1977. *Ethnic Chauvinism: The Reactionary Impulse*. New York: Stein and Day.

Paynter, Robert. 1981. "Social Complexity in Peripheries: Problems and Models," in *Archaeological Approaches to the Study of Complexity*, ed. S.E. van der Leeuw, pp. 118–141. Amsterdam.

Bibliography

Peattie, Roderick. 1944. *Look to the Frontiers: A Geography for the Peace Table.* Port Washington, NY: Kennikat Press.

Pellow, Deborah. 1996. "Introduction," in *Setting Boundaries: The Anthropology of Spatial and Social Organization,* ed. Deborah Pellow, pp. 1–8. Westport, CN: Bergin and Garvey.

Pitts, Martin, 2007. "The Emperor's New Clothes? The Utility of Identity in Roman Archaeology," *American Journal of Archaeology* 111:693–713.

Polanyi, Karl. 1944. *The Great Transformation: The Political and Economic Origins of Our Time.* Boston: Beacon Press.

_____, Conrad M. Arensberg, and Harry W. Pearson (eds.). 1957. *Trade and Market in the Early Empires: Economies in History and Theory.* Glencoe, IL: Free Press.

Poulaki-Pantermali, Eftichia. 1991. "I Anaskafes tou Olimbu," in *To Arheoloyiko Ergo sti Makedonia ke Thraki 2. 1988,* pp. 173–180. Thessaloniki: Ipuryio Makedonias-Thrakis, Ipuryio Politismu, Aristotelio Panepistimio Thessalonikis.

Pratt, Mary Louise. 1992. *Imperial Eyes: Travel Writing and Transculturation.* London: Routledge.

Price, John A. 1973. *Tijuana: Urbanization in a Border Culture.* Notre Dame: University of Notre Dame Press.

Ragin, Charles, and Daniel Chirot. 1984. "The World System of Immanuel Wallerstein: Sociology and Politics as History," in *Vision and Method in Historical Sociology,* ed. Theda Skocpol, pp. 276–312. Cambridge: Cambridge University Press.

Randsborg, Klavs. 1989. "The Town, the Power, and the Land: Denmark and Europe during the First Millennium AD," in *Centre and Periphery: Comparative Studies in Archaeology,* ed. Timothy C. Champion, pp. 207–226. London: Unwin Hyman.

_____. 1992. "Barbarians, Classical Antiquity and the Rise of Western Europe: An Archaeological Essay," *Past and Present* 137:8–24.

Raymond, Ann. 2005. "Importing Culture at Miletus: Minoans and Anatolians at Middle Bronze Age Miletus," in *Emporia: Aegeans in the Central and Eastern Mediterranean, Proceedings of the 10th International Aegean Conference/10e Rencontre égéenne internationale, Athens, Italian School of Archaeology, 14–18 April 2004,* ed. Robert Laffineur and Emanuele Greco, pp. 185–190. Aegaeum 25, Annales d'archéologie égéenne de l'Université de Liège et UT-PASP. Liège: Université de Liège, Histoire de l'art et archéologie de la Grece antique/University of Texas at Austin, Program in Aegean Scripts and Prehistory.

Redfield, Robert, Ralph Linton and Melville J. Herskovits. 1935. "A Memorandum for the Study of Acculturation," *Man* 35:145–148.

Reece, Richard. 1979. "Romano-British Interaction," in *Space, Hierarchy and Society: Interdisciplinary Studies in Social Area Analysis,* ed. Barry C. Burnham and John Kingsbury, pp. 229–240. BAR International Series 59. Oxford: British Archaeological Reports.

Renfrew, Colin. 1978. "Space, Time and Polity," in *The Evolution of Social Systems,* ed. J. Friedman and M.J. Rowlands, pp. 89–112. London: Duckworth.

_____. 1996. "Prehistory and the Identity of Europe: Or, Don't Let's Be Beastly to the Hungarians," in *Cultural Identity and Archaeology: The Construction of*

Bibliography

European Communities, ed. Paul Graves-Brown, Sian Jones and Clive Gamble, pp. 125–144. London: Routledge.
_____, and Eric V. Level. 1979. "Exploring Dominance: Predicting Polities from Centers," in *Transformations: Mathematical Approaches to Culture Change*, ed. Colin Renfrew and Kenneth L. Cooke, pp. 145–167. New York: Academic Press.

Revell, Louise. 2009. *Roman Imperialism and Local Identities*. Cambridge: Cambridge University Press.

Rice, Prudence M. 1998. "Contexts of Contact and Change: Peripheries, Frontiers, and Boundaries," in *Studies in Culture Contact: Interaction, Culture Change, and Archaeology*, ed. James G. Cusick, pp. 44–66. Center for Archaeological Investigations, Occasional Paper No. 25. Carbondale: Southern Illinois University.

Riley, Carroll L. 1982. *The Frontier People: The Greater Southwest in the Protohistoric Period*. Center for Archaeological Investigations Occasional Paper No. 1. Carbondale: Center for Archaeological Investigations, Southern Illinois University.

Rosman, Abraham, and Paula G. Rubel. 1998. *The Tapestry of Culture: An Introduction to Cultural Anthropology*, 6th ed. Boston: McGraw-Hill.

Ross, Jennie-Keith. 1975. "Social Borders: Definitions of Diversity," *Current Anthropology* 16: 53–72.

Rowlands, Michael, and Susan Frankenstein. 1998. "The Internal Structure and Regional Context of Early Iron Age Society in South-Western Germany," in *Social Transformations in Archaeology: Global and Local Perspectives*, ed. Kristian Kristiansen and Michael Rowlands, pp. 334–374. London: Routledge.

Roymans, Nico. 1983. "The North Belgic Tribes in the 1st Century B.C.: A Historical-Anthropological Perspective," in *Roman and Native in the Low Countries: Spheres of Interaction*, ed. Roel Brandt and Jan Slofstra, pp. 43–69. BAR International Series 184. Oxford: British Archaeological Reports.

Rutter, Jeremy B. 1993. "Review of Aegean Prehistory II: The Pre-Palatial Bronze Age of the Southern and Central Greek Mainland," *American Journal of Archaeology* 97: 745–797.

Sackett, James. 1990. "Style and Ethnicity in Archaeology: The Case for Isochrestism," in *The Uses of Style in Archaeology*, ed. Margaret Conkey and Christine Hastorf, pp. 32–43. Cambridge: Cambridge University Press.

Saddington, D.B. 1991. "The Parameters of Romanization," in *Roman Frontier Studies 1989: Proceedings of the XVth International Congress of Roman Frontier Studies*, ed. Valerie A. Maxfield and Michael J. Dobson, pp. 413–418. Exeter: University of Exeter Press.

Sahlins, Peter. 1989. *Boundaries: The Making of France and Spain in the Pyrenees*. Berkeley: University of California Press.

_____. 1990. "Natural Frontiers Revisited: France's Boundaries since the Seventeenth Century," *American Historical Review* 95:1423–1451.

Sampson, C. Garth. 1988. *Stylistic Boundaries among Mobile Hunter-Foragers*. Washington: Smithsonian Institution Press.

Sanderson, Stephen K. (ed.). 1995. *Civilizations and World Systems: Studying World-Historical Change*. Walnut Creek, CA: Altamira Press.

Bibliography

Sandstrom, Alan H. 1991. *Corn Is Our Blood: Culture and Ethnic Identity in a Contemporary Aztec Village.* Norman: University of Oklahoma Press.

Santley, Robert S., and Rani T. Alexander, 1992. "The Political Economy of Core-Periphery Systems," in *Resources, Power and Interregional Interaction,* ed. Edward M. Schortman and Patricia A. Urban, pp. 23–49. New York: Plenum Press.

Savage, William W., Jr., and Stephen I. Thompson. 1979. "The Comparative Study of the Frontier: An Introduction," in *The Frontier: Comparative Studies, Volume Two,* ed. William W. Savage, Jr. and Stephen I. Thompson, pp. 3–24. Norman: University of Oklahoma Press.

Schoep, Ilse. 2006. "Looking Beyond the First Palaces: Elites and the Agency of Power in EM III-MM II Crete," *American Journal of Archaeology* 110:37–64.

Schofield, Elizabeth. 1984. "Coming to Terms with Minoan Colonists," in *The Minoan Thalassocracy: Myth and Reality. Proceedings of the Third International Symposium at the Swedish Institute in Athens, 31 May–5 June 1982,* ed. Robin Hägg and Nanno Marinatos, pp. 45–47. Skrifter Utgivna av Svenska Institutet i Athen, 4, XXXII. Stockholm.

Schon, Robert, and Michael L. Galaty. 2006. "Diachronic Frontiers: Landscape Archaeology in Highland Albania," *Journal of World-Systems Research* 12: 231–262.

Schortman, Edward M., and Patricia A. Urban. 1987. "Modeling Interregional Interaction in Prehistory," in *Advances in Archaeological Method and Theory, Volume 11,* ed. Michael B. Schiffer, pp. 37–95. New York: Academic Press.

_____. 1992. "The Place of Interaction Studies in Archaeological Thought," in *Resources, Power and Interregional Interaction,* ed. Edward M. Schortman and Patricia A. Urban, pp. 3–21. New York: Plenum Press.

_____. 1994. "Living on the Edge: Core/Periphery Relations in Ancient Southeastern Mesoamerica," *Current Anthropology* 35:401–430.

Sellwood, Lyn. 1984. "Tribal Boundaries Viewed from the Perspective of Numismatic Evidence," in *Aspects of the Iron Age in Central Southern Britain,* ed. Barry Cunliffe and David Miles, pp. 191–204. Oxford: Oxford University Committee for Archaeology.

Service, Elman R. 1960. "The Law of Evolutionary Potential," in *Evolution and Culture,* ed. Marshall Sahlins and Elman R. Service, pp. 93–127. Ann Arbor: University of Michigan Press.

_____. 1962. *Primitive Social Organization: An Evolutionary Perspective.* New York: Random House.

Sharer, Robert J. 1977. "Lower Central America as Seen from Mesoamerica," in *Hunters, Gatherers and First Farmers Beyond Europe,* ed. J. V. S. Megaw, pp. 61–84. Leicester: Leicester University Press.

Shelton, Kim. 2010. "Mainland Greece," in *The Oxford Handbook of the Bronze Age Aegean,* ed. Eric H. Cline, pp. 139–148. Oxford: Oxford University Press.

Shennan, Stephen. 1989. "Introduction: Archaeological Approaches to Cultural Identity," in *Archaeological Approaches to Cultural Identity,* ed. Stephen Shennan, pp. 1–32. London: Unwin Hyman.

Sherratt, Susan. 1999. "E Pur Si Muove: Pots, Markets and Values in the Second Millennium Mediterranean," in *The Complex Past of Pottery: Production, Circulation and Consumption of Mycenaean and Greek Pottery (Sixteenth*

Bibliography

to Early Fifth Centuries BC). Proceedings of the ARCHON International Conference, Held in Amsterdam, 8–9 November 1996, ed. J.P. Crielaard, V. Stissi and G.J. van Wijngaarden, pp. 163–211. Amsterdam: J.C. Gieben.

Shils, Edward. 1975. "Center and Periphery," in *Center and Periphery: Essays in Macrosociology*, pp. 3–16. Chicago: The University of Chicago Press.

Shipley, Graham. 1993. "Distance, Development, Decline? World-Systems Analysis and the 'Hellenistic' World," in *Centre and Periphery in the Hellenistic World*, ed. Per Bilde, Troels Engberg-Pedersen, Lise Hannestad, Jan Zahle and Klavs Randsborg, pp. 271–284. Studies in Hellenistic Civilization IV. Aarhus: Aarhus University Press.

Siapkas, Johannes. 2003. *Heterological Ethnicity: Conceptualizing Identities in Ancient Greece*. Acta Universitatis Upsaliensis. Boreas. Uppsala Studies in Ancient Mediterranean and Near Eastern Civilizations 27. Uppsala, Sweden: University of Uppsala.

Sinopoli, Carla M. 1994. "The Archaeology of Empires," *Annual Review of Anthropology* 23:159–180.

Slofstra, Jan. 1983. "An Anthropological Approach to the Study of Romanization Processes," in *Roman and Native in the Low Countries: Spheres of Interaction*, ed. Roel Brandt and Jan Slofstra, pp. 71–104. BAR International Series 184. Oxford: British Archaeological Reports.

Smith, David M. 1990. "Introduction: The Sharing and Dividing of Geographical Space," in *Shared Space: Divided Space: Essays on Conflict and Territorial Organization*, ed. Michael Chisholm and David M. Smith, pp. 1–21. London: Unwin Hyman.

Smith, Henry Nash, 1950. "The Frontier Hypothesis and the Myth of the West," *American Quarterly* 2:3–11.

Smith, Stuart Tyson. 1998. "Nubia and Egypt: Interaction, Acculturation, and Secondary State Formation from the Third to First Millennium B.C.," in *Studies in Culture Contact: Interaction, Culture Change, and Archaeology*, ed. James G. Cusick, pp. 256–287. Center for Archaeological Investigations, Occasional Paper No. 25. Carbondale: Southern Illinois University.

Soja, Edward W. 1971. *The Political Organization of Space*. Commission on College Geography Resource Paper No. 8. Washington, D.C.: Association of American Geographers.

Sopher, David E. 1972. "Place and Location: Notes on the Spatial Patterning of Culture." *Social Science Quarterly* 53:321–337.

Speilmann, Katherine A. 1991. "Interaction Among Nonhierarchical Societies," in *Farmers, Hunters, and Colonists: Interaction between the Southwest and the Southern Plains*, ed. Katherine A. Spielmann, pp. 1–17. Tucson: University of Arizona Press.

Spence, Michael W. 2005. "A Zapotec Diaspora Network in Classic-Period Central Mexico, in *The Archaeology of Colonial Encounters*, ed. Gil J. Stein, pp.173–205. Santa Fe: School of American Research Press.

Spicer, Edward H. 1961. "Types of Contact and Processes of Change," in *Perspectives in American Indian Culture Change*, ed. Edward H. Spicer, pp. 517–544. Chicago: University of Chicago Press.

Stahl, Ann B. 1991. "Ethnic Style and Ethnic Boundaries: A Diachronic Case Study from West-Central Ghana," *Ethnohistory* 38: 50–75.

Stein, Gil J. 1998. "World System Theory and Alternative Modes of Interaction

Bibliography

in the Archaeology of Culture Contact," in *Studies in Culture Contact: Interaction, Culture Change, and Archaeology*, ed. James G. Cusick, pp. 220–255. Center for Archaeological Investigations, Occasional Paper No. 25. Carbondale: Southern Illinois University.

_____. 1999. *Rethinking World-Systems: Diasporas, Colonies and Interaction in Uruk Mesopotamia*. Tucson: The University of Arizona Press.

_____. 2005. "The Comparative Archaeology of Colonial Encounters," in *The Archaeology of Colonial Encounters: Comparative Perspectives*, ed. Gil J. Stein, pp. 3–31. Santa Fe: School of American Research.

Stone, Glenn Davis. 1992. "Social Distance, Spatial Relations, and Agricultural Production among the Kofyar of Namu District, Plateau State, Nigeria," *Journal of Anthropological Archaeology* 11:152–172.

Strassoldo, Raimondo. 1977. "The Study of Boundaries: A Systems-Oriented, Multi-Disciplinary, Bibliographical Essay," *Jerusalem Journal of International Relations* 2:81–107.

_____. 1980. "Centre-Periphery and System-Boundary: Culturological Perspectives," in *Centre and Periphery: Spatial Variation in Politics*, ed. Jean Gottman, pp. 27–61. Beverly Hills: Sage Publications.

Szynkiewicz, Slawoj. 1989. "Interactions between the Nomadic Cultures of Central Asia and China in the Middle Ages," in *Centre and Periphery: Comparative Studies in Archaeology*, ed. Timothy C. Champion, pp. 151–158. London: Unwin Hyman.

Tambs-Lyche, Harald. 1994. "Ethnic Groups and Boundaries: Nordic Schools of Approach," in *Inventions and Boundaries: Historical and Anthropological Approaches to the Study of Ethnicity and Nationalism: Papers from the Researcher Training Course Held at Sandbjerg Manor, 23 to 29 May 1993*, ed. Preben Kaarsholm and Jun Hultin, pp. 51–73. Roskilde University International Development Studies Occasional Paper No. 11. Roskilde, Denmark.

Tartaron, Thomas F. 2001. "Glykys Limin: A Mycenaean Port of Trade in Southern Epirus?" in *Prehistory and History: Ethnicity, Class and Political Economy*, ed. David W. Tandy, pp. 1–40. Montreal: Black Rose Books.

_____. 2004. *Bronze Age Society and Landscape in Southern Epirus, Greece*. BAR International Series 1290. Oxford: Archaeopress.

_____. 2005. "Glykys Limin and the Discontinuous Mycenaean Periphery," in *Emporia: Aegeans in the Central and Eastern Mediterranean. Proceedings of the 10th International Aegean Conference/10ᵉ Rencontre égéenne internationale, Athens, Italian School of Archaeology, 14–18 April 2004*, ed. Robert Laffineur and Emanuele Greco, pp. 153–160. Aegaeum 25, Annales d'archéologie égéenne de l'Université de Liège et UT-PASP. Liège: Université de Liège, Histoire de l'art et archéologie de la Grece antique/University of Texas at Austin, Program in Aegean Scripts and Prehistory.

Theodossopoulos, Dimitrios. 2003. "Degrading Others and Honouring Ourselves: Ethnic Stereotypes as Categories and as Explanations," *Journal of Mediterranean Studies* 13: 177–188.

Thomas, Peter A. 1985. "Cultural Change on the Southern New England Frontier, 1630–1665," in *Cultures in Contact: The Impact of European Contacts on Native American Cultural Institutions, A.D. 1000–1800*, ed. William W. Fitzhugh, pp. 131–161. Anthropological Society of Washington Series. Washington, D.C.: Smithsonian Institution Press.

Bibliography

Thompson, Leonard. 1983. "The Southern African Frontier in Comparative Perspective," in *Essays on Frontiers in World History*, ed. George Wolfskill and Stanley Palmer, pp. 101–134. College Station: Texas A&M Press.
_____, and Howard Lamar. 1981. "Comparative Frontier History," in *The Frontier in History: North America and Southern Africa Compared*, ed. Howard Lamar and Leonard Thompson, pp. 3–13. New Haven: Yale University Press.
Thornton, Robert. 1982. "Modelling of Spatial Relations in a Boundary-Marking Ritual of the Iraqw of Tanzania," *Man* 17:528–545.
Tiruchelvam, Mithran. 1996. "Crossing the Boundary: The Framing of a Qing Political Community in Frontier Taiwan," *China Report* 32: 101–118.
Trigger, Bruce G. 1974. "The Archaeology of Government," *World Archaeology* 6:95–105.
_____. 1977. "Comments on Archaeological Classification and Ethnic Groups," *Norwegian Archaeological Review* 10:20–23.
_____. 1984. "Archaeology at the Crossroads: What's New?" *Annual Review of Anthropology* 13:275–300.
Trinkaus, Kathryn Maurer. 1984. "Boundary Maintenance Strategies and Archaeological Indicators," in *Exploring the Limits: Frontiers and Boundaries in Prehistory*, ed. Suzanne P. De Atley and Frank J. Findlow, pp. 35–49. BAR International Series 223. Oxford: British Archaeological Reports
Triulzi, Alessandro. 1994. "Ethiopia: The Making of a Frontier Society," in *Inventions and Boundaries: Historical and Anthropological Approaches to the Study of Ethnicity and Nationalism: Papers from the Researcher Training Course held at Sandbjerg Manor, 23 to 29 May 1993*, ed. Preben Kaarsholm and Jun Hultin, pp. 235–245. Roskilde University International Development Studies Occasional Paper No. 11. Roskilde, Denmark.
Tsetskhladze, Gocha R. 2006. "Revisiting Ancient Greek Colonisation." in *Greek Colonisation: An Account of Greek Colonies and Other Settlements Overseas, Volume 1*, ed. Gocha R. Tsetskhladze, pp. xxiii-lxxxiii. Leiden: Brill.
Turner, Frederick Jackson. 1893. "The Significance of the Frontier in American History," *Annual Reports of the American Historical Association*, 199–207.
Tweddell, Colin E. 1978. "The Tuli-Chinese Balk Line: Minimal Group Self-Identity," in *Perspectives on Ethnicity*, ed. Regina E. Holloman and Serghei A. Arutiunov, pp. 301–325. The Hague: Mouton Publishers.
Ucko, Peter J. 1989. "Forward," in *Centre and Periphery: Comparative Studies in Archaeology*, ed. Timothy C. Champion, pp. ix-xvi. London: Unwin Hyman.
Urban, Patricia A., and Edward M. Schortman. 1988. "The Southeast Zone Viewed from the East: Lower Motagua-Naco Valleys," in *The Southeast Classic Maya Zone: A Symposium at Dumbarton Oaks, 6th and 7th October 1984*, ed. Elizabeth Hill Boone and Gordon R. Willey, pp. 223–267. Washington, D.C.: Dumbarton Oaks Research Library and Collection.
van der Leeuw, Sander E. 1983. "Acculturation as Information Processing," in *Roman and Native in the Low Countries: Spheres of Interaction*, ed. Roel Brandt and Jan Slofstra, pp. 11–41. BAR International Series 184. Oxford: British Archaeological Reports.
van Dommelen, Peter. 2005. "Colonial Interactions and Hybrid Practices: Phoenician and Carthaginian Settlement in the Ancient Mediterranean," in *The Archaeology of Colonial Encounters*, ed. Gil J. Stein, pp.109–141. Santa Fe: School of American Research Press.

Bibliography

_____. 2006. "The Orientalizing Phenomenon: Hybridity and Material Culture in the Western Mediterranean," in *Debating Orientalization: Multidisciplinary Approaches to Change in the Ancient Mediterranean*, ed. Corinna Riva and Nicholas C. Vella, pp. 135–152. London: Equinox Publishing Ltd.

van Wijngaarden, Gert Jan. 2001. "The Cultural Significance of Mycenaean Pictorial Kraters," *Pharos* 9:75–95.

Varberg, Jeannette. 2007 "Dawn of a New Age: The Late Neolithic as Third Space," in *Encounters / Materialities / Confrontations: Archaeologies of Social Space and Interaction*, ed. P. Cornell and F. Fahlander, pp. 58–82. Newcastle: Cambridge Scholars Press.

Vianello, Andrea. 2005. *Late Bronze Age Mycenaean and Italic Products in the West Mediterranean: A Social and Economic Analysis*. BAR International Series 1439. Oxford: Archaeopress.

Vives-Ferrándiz, Jaime. 2008. "Negotiating Colonial Encounters: Hybrid Practices and Consumption in Eastern Iberia (8th-6th centuries BC)," *Journal of Mediterranean Archaeology* 21:241–272.

Voskos, Ioannis, and A. Bernard Knapp. 2008. "Cyprus at the End of the Late Bronze Age: Crisis and Colonization or Continuity and Hybridization?" *American Journal of Archaeology* 112:659–684.

Voutsaki, Sofia. 2001. "The Rise of Mycenae: Political Inter-Relations and Archaeological Evidence," *Bulletin of the Institute of Classical Studies* 45: 183–184.

_____. 2010. "Mainland Greece," in *The Oxford Handbook of the Bronze Age Aegean*, ed. Eric H. Cline, pp. 99–112. Oxford: Oxford University Press.

Wagner, Philip L. 1988. "Why Diffusion?" in *The Transfer and Transformation of Ideas and Material Culture*, ed. Peter J. Hugill and D. Bruce Dickson, pp. 179–193. College Station: Texas A&M Press.

Waller, Richard. 1993. "Acceptees & Aliens: Kikuyu Settlement in Maasailand," in *Being Maasai: Ethnicity & Identity in East Africa*, ed. Thomas Spear and Richard Walker, pp. 226–257. London: James Currey.

Wallerstein, Immanuel. 1974. *The Modern World-System I: Capitalist Agriculture and the Origin of the European World-Economy in the Sixteenth Century*. New York: Academic Press.

Wallman, Sandra. 1978. "The Boundaries of 'Race': Processes of Ethnicity in England," *Man* 13:200–217.

Watson, James B. 1990. "Other People Do Other Things: Lamarckian Identities in Kainantu Subdistrict, Papua New Guinea," in *Cultural Identity and Ethnicity in the Pacific*, ed. Jocelyn Linnekin and Lin Poyer pp. 17–41. Honolulu: University of Hawaii.

Webb, Walter Prescott. 1952. *The Great Frontier*. Boston: Houghton Mifflin Company.

Weber, David J. 1982. *The Mexican Frontier, 1821–1846: The American Southwest under Mexico*. Albuquerque: University of New Mexico Press.

_____. 1986. "Turner, the Boltonians, and the Borderlands," *The American Historical Review* 91:66–81.

_____. 1992. *The Spanish Frontier in North America*. New Haven: Yale University Press.

_____, and Jane M. Rausch. 1994. "Introduction," in *Where Cultures Meet: Frontiers in Latin American History*, David J. Weber and Jane M. Rausch, eds.,

Bibliography

pp. xiii-xli. Jaguar Books on Latin America, Number 6. Wilmington, DE: Scholarly Resources, Inc.

Webster, Jane. 2001. "Creolizing Roman Britain," *American Journal of Archaeology* 105:209–225.

Wells, Peter S. 1980. *Culture Contact and Culture Change: Early Iron Age Central Europe and the Mediterranean World.* Cambridge: Cambridge University Press.

_____. 1987. "Sociopolitical Change and Core-Periphery Interactions: An Example from Early Iron Age Europe," in *Polities and Partitions: Human Boundaries and the Growth of Complex Societies,* ed. Kathryn Maurer Trinkaus, pp. 141–155. Arizona State University Anthropological Research Papers No. 37.

_____. 1992. "Tradition, Identity, and Change beyond the Roman Frontier," in *Resources, Power and Interregional Interaction,* ed. Edward M. Schortman and Patricia A. Urban, pp. 175–187. New York: Plenum Press.

_____. 1998. "Culture Contact, Identity, and Change in the European Provinces of the Roman Empire," in *Studies in Culture Contact: Interaction, Culture Change, and Archaeology,* ed. James G. Cusick, pp. 316–334. Center for Archaeological Investigations, Occasional Paper No. 25. Carbondale: Southern Illinois University.

_____. 2001. *Beyond Celts, Germans and Scythians: Archaeology and Identity in Iron Age Europe.* London: Duckworth.

Wells, Robin F. 1973. "Frontier Systems as a Sociocultural Type," *Papers in Anthropology* 14:6–15.

White, Richard. 1991. *The Middle Ground: Indians, Empires, and Republics in the Great Lakes Region, 1650–1815.* Cambridge: Cambridge University Press.

Whitecotton, Joseph W., and Richard A. Pailes. 1986. "New World Precolumbian World Systems," in *Ripples in the Chichimec Sea: New Considerations of Southwestern-Mesoamerican Interactions,* ed. Frances Joan Mathien and Randall H. McGuire, pp. 183–204. Carbondale: Southern Illinois University Press.

Whitney, Joseph B.R. 1970. *China: Area, Administration, and Nation.* Research Paper no. 123. University of Chicago Department of Geography.

Whittaker, C.R. 1983. "Trade and Frontiers of the Roman Empire," in *Trade and Famine in Classical Antiquity,* ed. Peter Garnsey and C.R. Whittaker, pp. 110–127. Cambridge Philological Society Supplementary Volume no. 8. Cambridge: Cambridge Philological Society.

_____. 1989. "Supplying the System: Frontiers and Beyond," in *Barbarians and Romans in North-West Europe: From the Later Republic to Late Antiquity,* ed. John C. Barrett, Andrew P. Fitzpatrick and Lesley Macinnes, pp. 64–80. BAR International Series 471. Oxford: British Archaeological Reports.

_____. 1993. "What Happens When Frontiers Come to an End?" in *Frontières d'Empire: Nature et Signification des Frontières romaines. Actes de la Table Ronde Internationale de Nemours, 21–22–23 Mai 1992,* ed. Patrice Brun, Sander van der Leeuw and Charles R. Whittaker, pp. 133–140. Nemours: Ouvrage Publiè avec le Concours du Centre National de la Recherche Scientifique, du Conseil Gènèral de Seine-et Marne et de la Ville de Nemours.

_____. 1994. *Frontiers of the Roman Empire: A Social and Economic Study.* Baltimore: The Johns Hopkins University Press.

Wiessner, Polly. 1989. "Style and Changing Relations Between the Individual and

Bibliography

Society," in *The Meanings of Things: Material Culture and Symbolic Expression*, ed. Ian Hodder, pp. 56–63. London: Unwin Hyman.

Wilkie, Nancy C. 1999. "Some aspects of the Prehistoric Occupation of Grevena," in Αρχαία Μακεδονία VI, Ανακοινώσεις κατά το Έκτο Διεθνές Συμπόσιο, Θεσσαλονίκη, 15–19 Οκτωβρίου 1996. *Ancient Macedonia VI, Papers Read at the Sixth International Symposium Held in Thessaloniki, October 15–19, 1996*, Παντερμαλής, Volume 2, ed. B. Κόντης, A. Βαβρίτσας, E. Βουτυράς and I. Τουλουμάκος, pp. 1345–1357. Institute for Balkan Studies 272. Thessaloniki: Institute for Balkan Studies.

Wilkinson, David. 1991. "Cores, Peripheries and Civilizations," in *Core/Periphery Relations in Precapitalist Worlds*, ed. Christopher Chase-Dunn and Thomas D. Hall, pp. 113–166. Boulder: Westview Press.

Wilkinson, John C. 1983. "Traditional Concepts of Territory in South East Arabia," *The Geographical Journal* 149:301–315.

Willems, Willem J.H. 1983. "Romans and Batavians: Regional Developments at the Imperial Frontier," in *Roman and Native in the Low Countries: Spheres of Interaction*, ed. Roel Brandt and Jan Slofstra, pp. 105–128. BAR International Series 184, Oxford: British Archaeological Reports.

Willey, Gordon R., Charles C. Di Peso, William A. Ritchie, Irving Rouse, John H. Rowe and Donald W. Lathrap. 1956. "An Archaeological Classification of Culture Contact Situations," in *Seminars in Archaeology: 1955*, ed. Robert Wauchope, pp. 5–30. Memoirs of the Society for American Archaeology, Number 11. Salt Lake City: The Society for American Archaeology.

Williams, Derek. 1998. *Romans and Barbarians: Four Views from the Empire's Edge 1st Century AD*. New York: St. Martin's Press.

Winks, Robin W. 1983. "Australia, the Frontier, and the Tyranny of Distance," in *Essays on Frontiers in World History*, ed. George Wolfskill and Stanley Palmer, pp. 135–165. College Station: Texas A&M Press.

Wobst, H.M. 1977. *Stylistic Behavior and Information Exchange*. University of Michigan Museum of Anthropology, Anthropological Paper 61, pp. 317–342.

Wolf, Eric R. 1982. *Europe and the People without History*. Berkeley: University of California Press.

Wonderley, Anthony. 1986. "Naco, Honduras—Some Aspects of a Late Precolumbian Community on the Eastern Maya Frontier," in *The Southeast Maya Periphery*, ed. Patricia A. Urban and Edward M. Schortman, pp. 313–332. Austin: University of Texas Press.

Woolf, Greg. 1990. "World-Systems Analysis and the Roman Empire," *Journal of Roman Archaeology* 3:44–58.

_____. 1998. *Becoming Roman: The Origins of Provincial Civilization in Gaul*. Cambridge: Cambridge University Press.

Wright, James C. (ed). 2004. *The Mycenaean Feast*. Princeton: American School of Classical Studies at Athens.

_____. 2008. "Early Mycenaean Greece," in *The Cambridge Companion to the Aegean Bronze Age*, ed. Cynthia W. Shelmerdine, pp. 230–257. Cambridge: Cambridge University Press.

Wright, Rita P. 1987. "The Frontiers of Prehistoric Baluchistan and the Development of the Indus Civilization," in *Polities and Partitions: Human Boundaries and the Growth of Complex Societies*, ed. Kathryn Maurer Trinkaus,

Bibliography

pp. 61–82. Arizona State University Anthropological Research Papers No. 37.

Wu, Xiaolong. 2013. "Cultural Hybridity and Social Status: Elite Tombs on China's Northern Frontier during the Third Century BC," *Antiquity* 87:121–136.

Wyman, Walker D., and Clifton B. Kroeber. 1965. "Introduction," in *The Frontier in Perspective*, ed. Walker D. Wyman and Clifton B. Kroeber, pp. xiii-xx. Madison: University of Wisconsin Press.

Yinger, J. Milton. 1985. "Ethnicity," *Annual Review of Sociology* 11:151–180.

Zenner, Walter P. 1978. "Jewish Communities as Cultural Units," in *Perspectives on Ethnicity*, ed. Regina E. Holloman and Serghei A. Arutiunov, pp. 327–338. The Hague: Mouton Publishers.

Index

accommodation 22
acculturation 8, 72–78, 84–89, 95–96, 100–102, 107, 110, 115, 117, 119; differential 75, 117–118; partial 74–75, 85, 88, 95, 101, 110, 119; *see also* diffusion; Mycenaeanization; Romanization
adapted spread 39
Aegean Sea 66, 106–108
agency 23, 75; *see also* consumption
agriculture 7–8, 38–40, 44–45, 55, 58, 60, 62, 65–66, 92–94, 109, 114; *see also* domestication; sedentism
archaeological culture 4, 24–27, 35, 84
Argissa 113
assimilation 8, 20, 34, 74, 76–77, 81, 84, 87–89, 93, 101, 119

barbarism 5, 86, 95, 103–104; *see also* civilization
Bhabha, Homi 22; *see also* third space
border 3, 8–9, 11, 14–15, 46, 52–54, 57, 60, 62–63, 89, 93, 95–96, 99, 102, 110, 113, 115, 117, 119–120; *see also* periphery; semi-periphery
boundary 3–5, 7, 11–14, 35–37, 42–44, 46, 56, 62, 83, 87–88, 102–104; natural 4, 13, 51–52, 56, 103; political 8, 37, 51–52, 56, 87; social 8, 13, 83–85
Bronze Age 9, 25, 31, 47, 61, 66, 105–120
buffer zone 7–8, 21, 42–45, 52–54, 58, 66, 100, 102

Caesar, Julius 96–97
center 3, 5–6, 9, 12, 15, 18, 27–35, 48–50, 56–58, 61–62, 65, 91, 95–96, 120; *see also* core zone

central place theory 4, 37
centralization 4, 33, 42, 46–49
ceremonial feasting 55, 76–77, 86, 107, 116, 119; *see also* commensal politics
chiefdom 4, 7, 21, 45–46, 49, 97, 100, 105, 113; *see also* tribe
Childe, V. Gordon 26
Ch'in 91
China 62, 66–67, 90–95, 103–105
cist grave 117
civilization 5, 86, 94–95; *see also* barbarism
Clarke, David 26; *see also* polythetic assemblage
colonialism 21–22, 29, 62, 73; *see also* imperialism
colonization 17, 21, 22, 38–40, 72, 74; gradient 40
colony 20–21, 29, 64, 89
commensal politics 55, 77; *see also* ceremonial feasting
comparative frontiers 19, 38, 40, 104
conflict 9, 45, 49, 52, 55–57, 96; *see also* warfare
consumption 74; *see also* agency
contact zone 21, 71; *see also* interaction
contested ground 22
core zone 2–5, 7, 14–15, 18, 27–35, 39, 43, 49, 54–55, 65, 84, 91–92, 94, 96, 99, 105, 109–113, 115, 117–119; *see also* center
Costion, Kirk 40
craft production 60, 65
creolization 8, 76, 84; *see also* hybridity; syncretism
Crete 105–106, 111–112
culture contact 70–78; *see also* interaction

153

Index

Index